Cost Effectiveness in Medical Education

Cost Effectiveness in Medical Education

Edited by

KIERAN WALSH

MB, BCH, BAO, DCH, FHEA, FRCPI, FAcadMed
Editor
BMJ Learning

Foreword by

Sir Liam Donaldson

Chief Medical Officer
1998–2010

Radcliffe Publishing
Oxford • New York

Radcliffe Publishing Ltd
18 Marcham Road
Abingdon
Oxon OX14 1AA
United Kingdom

www.radcliffepublishing.com

Electronic catalogue and worldwide online ordering facility.

British Library Cataloguing in Publication Data

A catalogue record for this book is available from the British Library.

ISBN-13: 978 184619 410 8

The paper used for the text pages of this book is FSC certified. FSC (The Forest Stewardship Council) is an international network to promote responsible management of the world's forests.

Mixed Sources
Product group from well-managed forests and other controlled sources
www.fsc.org Cert no. SGS-COC-2482
© 1996 Forest Stewardship Council

Typeset by KnowledgeWorks Global Ltd, Chennai, India
Printed and bound by TJI Digital, Padstow, Cornwall, UK

Contents

Foreword

Ever since Archie Cochrane's *Random Reflections*, clinicians have been exhorted to practice 'evidence-based' medicine. All interventions to treat patients are supposed to be assessed on both their effectiveness and efficiency. The intention being that through a process of careful evaluation and critical appraisal, only treatments that provide real benefit will be offered and those that are not beneficial or even harmful can be identified and stopped. Paradoxically, calls to similarly assess the means used to train the doctors who will carry out these carefully evaluated interventions have been rather muted.

There are clearly difficulties in evaluating a process that occurs over such a long period of time. Despite these difficulties, there have been significant efforts made to appraise the teaching methods employed in our medical schools. To date, these have tended to focus on the former of Cochrane's criteria, effectiveness. Researchers have an increasingly good knowledge of what general outcomes can be expected of different approaches to medical education. Until this book, the second criteria, efficiency, has been largely overlooked.

Many millions of pounds are spent in medical schools each year to train the doctors of the future. The intention has always been to produce excellent doctors. Anything less is simply unacceptable. Allowing poorly trained doctors to practice would risk medical errors and worse outcomes, ultimately costing the lives of patients. Perhaps this pursuit of excellence has deflected us from seriously examining the cost of medical education. As long as the end result was good enough, and to date it has been excellent, any price was a price worth paying.

In the current, cost-constrained environment, those funding the education of our doctors will no longer tolerate an approach of quality at any cost. Different methods of medical education will inevitably carry different costs and produce different outcomes. Without critical examination of each option, it is impossible to select those that give optimum outcomes at acceptable cost. The cost effectiveness of each method will become increasing scrutinised as investors seek the greatest return.

This book represents a systematic attempt to examine this investment. The good news is that cost-effective does not have to mean lower quality; far from it. With increasing study and understanding of medical education, effective methods can be improved, while the ineffective are left behind. If an assessment of efficiency is combined with this, medical education can be made smarter and more focussed on what works and the same high standards attained at a lower overall cost. The harnessing of new techniques and technology is likely to become increasingly important, e-learning and simulation being good examples.

There is an increasing responsibility on us all to examine our practice and be prepared to engage in efforts to examine and improve cost effectiveness. It is only in doing this in medical education that we can ensure that we continue to provide excellence in our medical schools and produce excellent doctors for generations to come.

This book is an excellent analysis and explanation of an under-explored subject and will be of great value to policy makers and medical educators.

Sir Liam Donaldson
Chief Medical Officer 1998–2010
June 2010

About the editor

Dr Kieran Walsh is Editor of *BMJ Learning*—the education service of the BMJ Group. He is responsible for the strategic directions of the online learning service and for BMJ Masterclasses—face-to-face learning meetings and for Onexamination—the exam support product. He has written more than 200 articles for publication, mainly in the field of medical education. He has worked in the past as a hospital doctor, specialising in care of the elderly medicine and neurology.

List of contributors

CHAPTER 2

Professor Paul Finucane, FRCPI, FRACP, is foundation head of the Graduate Entry Medical School, University of Limerick, Ireland. He was formerly director of education at the Medical Council of Ireland and previously was professor and assistant dean at the School of Medicine at Flinders University, Adelaide, South Australia. He has also worked in clinical medicine and in medical education in other parts of Ireland and Australia, as well as in Wales and in the Middle East. His clinical background is in Geriatric Medicine and in Medical Rehabilitation. He has published extensively, has edited three textbooks and has written several book chapters.

Peter McCrorie, BSc, PhD, is professor of Medical Education at St George's University of London, United Kingdom. He is head of the Centre for Medical and Healthcare Education, director of the 4-year MBBS Graduate Entry Programme and associate dean for International Affairs. He is an Associate of the UK General Medical Council (GMC) and carries out quality assurance of basic medical undergraduate programmes in UK medical schools. He works extensively on curriculum development with universities in countries across the world, including Brunei, Malta, Portugal, Australia, Cyprus and Ireland. His research interests lie in curriculum development, assessment, graduate entry, self-directed and problem-based learning, community-oriented medical education, interprofessional learning and staff development.

CHAPTER 3

Dr Hemal Thakore, MA, MSc, MD, FAcadMed, is an independent medical education specialist who has worked for a number of universities and institutions in a senior medical education capacity. He is currently working with the recently formed Irish College of Psychiatry as a medical education specialist developing a competency-based postgraduate training programme. His major interests in medical education are educational leadership, educational programme reform and development and the teaching of professionalism within the curriculum. He read medicine at Trinity College Dublin and continues to maintain a clinical component as part of his professional career.

CHAPTERS 4 AND 6

Dr John Sandars, MB ChB (Hons), MSc, MD, MRCP, FRCGP, FHEA, FAcadMed, Cert Ed, is senior lecturer in Community Based Education, Academic Lead for e-learning, Medical Education Unit, Leeds Institute of Medical Education, United Kingdom. He has a major research and development interest in the use of technology to enhance teaching and learning in both undergraduate and postgraduate medical education. He has published numerous articles about e-learning and is a regular commentator on this area for *Education for Primary Care*. He has previously been a GP trainer and GP tutor.

CHAPTER 5

Debra Nestel, PhD, is professor of Medical Education, Gippsland Medical School, Monash University, Victoria, Australia, where her main curriculum responsibilities are in programme evaluation. For more than 20 years, she has taught and researched clinical communication in medicine and in new health professional roles. She has published more than 100 peer-reviewed papers, many with a focus on simulation as an educational method. She has a degree in sociology and a doctorate in programme evaluation and clinical communication. She has worked at the University of Hong Kong and Imperial College.

Brett Williams, BAVEd, Grad Cert ICP, Grad Dip EmergHlth, MHlthSc, MACAP, is a senior lecturer in the Department of Community Emergency Health and Paramedic Practice, Monash University. He has 16 years experience in paramedic education and training and has taught and developed curricula for both undergraduate and postgraduate students in both face-to-face and e-learning modes. He is undertaking his PhD, which is developing a valid and reliable graduate attribute scale for undergraduate paramedic students. His research interests are focused on the paradigm of student-centred learning, educational technology, interprofessional education, test development and evaluation, and applications of the Rasch Measurement Model.

Professor Elmer Villanueva, MD, ScM, is associate professor of Public Health and director of Research at the Gippsland Medical School, Monash University, Victoria, Australia. He is responsible for the establishment of a population health research and teaching programme and participates in the development of regional population health research activity. He has held senior research posts at policy organisations and universities, where his work has focused on population health, epidemiologic methodology, biostatistics and evidence-based medicine.

CHAPTER 7

Professor John Spencer, MBChB, FRCGP, FAcadMedEd, is professor of Medical Education, sub-dean for Primary and Community Care, and director of Research and Development at Newcastle University, Newcastle upon Tyne, United Kingdom. A general practitioner by trade, he has been involved in healthcare professional education for more than 25 years in a wide range of settings, predominantly undergraduate medical education. He has also been an active researcher, in both health services and healthcare professional education research, and has published extensively. He was deputy editor of *Medical Education* for 11 years and editor-in-chief of *The Clinical Teacher* for 4 years. He has held numerous positions as external examiner, consultant and adviser, and has worked with a variety of organisations and agencies such as the General Medical Council, Quality Assurance Agency and the Higher Education Agency Subject Centres. His research interests include the role of the patient in medical education and evaluation of clinical teaching. He is a long-suffering Newcastle United season ticket holder.

John Pearson is clinical placement and finance manager for the MBBS programme at Newcastle Medical School—a post formally known as 'SIFT Coordinator'. His primary role is to ensure that money allocated to support undergraduate medical education and training is distributed according to activity. In this role, he works closely with the North East Strategic Health Authority, which holds the Multi Professional Education and Training resources. As part of the Strategic Health Authority quality monitoring team, he is heavily involved in evaluating the student experience during clinical attachments. In addressing issues of programme delivery and quality management, he is a member of many of the Medical School curriculum management groups.

CHAPTER 8

Dr Jean Ker, BSc, MD, DRCOG, FRCGP, FRCPE, FHEA, is director of the Institute of Health Skills and Education, College of Medicine, Dentistry and Nursing, University of Dundee, and is the lead clinician for the Scottish Clinical Skills Managed Education Network responsible for ensuring that high standards of skills education are available to all healthcare practitioners. This has led to a 2-year pilot of a mobile clinical skills resource using standardised evidence-based resources. She founded the Scottish Clinical Skills Network and has developed an innovative prize-winning ward simulation exercise. She has written more than 70 articles, including editorials, original research, book chapters and reviews.

George Hogg, MSc, BN, DANS, RGN, PGCTHE, FHEA, is lecturer in Interprofessional Clinical Skills, College of Medicine, Dentistry and Nursing, University of Dundee. His background is in acute and critical care nursing and was previously a transfusion nurse specialist where he developed his interest in clinical risk management and teaching. He is currently completing an EdD looking at the development of a simulation-based course on patient safety and the deteriorating patient.

Dr Nicola Maran, FRCA, FRCSEd, is a consultant anaesthetist and part-time senior lecturer in the Royal Infirmary of Edinburgh and is director of the Scottish Clinical Simulation Centre in Stirling. Her specialist interests are in patient safety, human factors and nontechnical skills and in the use of simulation for training and assessment.

CHAPTER 9

Professor Gary Wittert, MBBch, MD, FRACP, FRCP, is a graduate of the University of Witwatersrand, Johannesburg, South Africa, and is currently head, Discipline of Medicine, The University of Adelaide, Australia, and senior consultant endocrinologist, Royal Adelaide Hospital. He has a longstanding interest in systems of clinical training, including design of clinical curricula, systems of integrating basic sciences and clinical skills, clinical reasoning and online learning. He is a chief investigator in the NH&MRC Centre of Clinical Research Excellence for Nutritional Physiology, founding member of the Freemasons Foundation Centre for Men's Health Research and initiated and oversees the Florey Adelaide Male Ageing Study. He is the independent chair of the Weight Management Council of Australia and vice president of the Asia Oceania Society for the Study of Obesity. His research is undertaken at basic, clinical and population health levels. He has authored more than 150 peer-reviewed journal articles and book chapters.

Adam Nelson, BMedSc (Hons), is a final-year medical student at the University of Adelaide. He has completed a BMedSc (Hons) degree in cardiovascular medicine and has a keen interest in both cardiovascular research and medical education. He has been extensively involved in the curriculum committees at the University of Adelaide and has developed a peer-tutoring programme at the medical school.

CHAPTERS 10 AND 13

Dr Rodney Gale, DPhil, MBA, is an honorary fellow in management at the Open University Centre for Education in Medicine and a freelance consultant. He has spent most of his paid career in research and research governance but has maintained an interest in medical education and medical management. He has run numerous courses on management for clinical tutors and clinical directors. His formal business training was at the London Business School and his most recent NHS role was as director of Research Support at Imperial College Healthcare NHS Trust.

Professor Janet Grant, BA, MSc, PhD, FBPsS, CPsychol, is director of the Open University Centre for Education at the Open University, Walton Hall, Milton Keynes, United

Kingdom, where she and her team conduct policy research in medical education. She is a special adviser to the World Federation for Medical Education (WFME) and works closely with the Foundation for the Advancement of International Medical Education and Research (FAIMER) of the US Educational Commission for Foreign Medical Graduates. With WFME and FAIMER, the Open University Centre for Education in Medicine team delivers international distance learning modules in medical education. She was a foundation member of the UK regulatory body for postgraduate medical education, the Postgraduate Medical Education and Training Board and chair of its Curriculum Sub-Committee. She is a member of the Education and Training Committee of the Solicitors Regulation Authority and the Joint Academic Standards Board of the Bar Council.

CHAPTER 11

Professor Lambert Schuwirth, MD, PhD, is professor for Innovative Assessment in medical education, Department of Educational Development and Research, Maastricht University, The Netherlands. He is leader of the task force Assessment at the faculty of health, medicine and life sciences at Maastricht University in the Netherlands. He is and has been adviser to various royal colleges, the general medical council and medical schools in the United Kingdom in matters of assessment. In the Netherlands, he has been a member of several national committees on assessment, such as the committee for the assessment of foreign medical graduates and the interuniversity progress test committee (which he chaired for more than 5 years). His research focuses on assessment in the context of an educational programme, assessment for learning.

Professor Cees van der Vleuten, PhD, is professor of Education, Director School of Health Professions Education, Chair Department of Educational Development and Research, Faculty of Health, Medicine and Life Sciences, Maastricht University, Maastricht, The Netherlands. His area of expertise lies in evaluation and assessment. His particular expertise concerns assessment of professional competence, including modern methods of assessment and strategies for designing assessment programmes. He has published widely on these topics, holds numerous academic awards for this work and has been a mentor for many PhD students. He has frequently served as a consultant internationally. He has held honourable appointments to a number of universities throughout the world.

CHAPTER 12

Dr John Goldie, MMEd, MD, FRCGP, FHEA, is a full-time GP, vocational studies tutor and senior clinical tutor in the Section of General Practice & Primary Care at the University of Glasgow. His research interests are in the fields of educational evaluation and professionalism and ethics teaching. He has 18 publications including 10 original articles and three review articles.

CHAPTER 14

Dr Melanie Calvert, PhD, is senior lecturer, Health Care Evaluation Group, School of Health and Population Sciences, Primary Care and Clinical Sciences Building, University of Birmingham, Edgbaston, Birmingham. She is experienced in the design and analysis of clinical trials and epidemiology and has researched across a range of clinical disciplines including diabetes and heart failure. She provides research-informed teaching to University students, clinicians, members of industry, and PhD supervision and is the Education Lead for the MRC Midland Hub for Trials Methodology Research. She is a fellow of the Higher Education Academy and is currently involved in a range of collaborative projects that aim to provide evidence to inform medical education. She has published more than 40 peer-reviewed papers including work in the *BMJ* and *JAMA*.

CHAPTER 1

Cost effectiveness in medical education: an introduction

Kieran Walsh

The man in the street is highly sceptical of the value of cost-effectiveness analysis: their unpopularity is scarcely surprising, if only because when beliefs come into conflict with evidence, beliefs tend to win.

—Drummond Rennie

Medical education is an expensive business. It takes hundreds of thousands of pounds to educate each medical student to a state where he or she is fit to become a doctor and start work. And on day 2, the new doctor will start his or her postgraduate education, which may take another 10 years. Then, there is another 30 years of continuing professional development until retirement. Each year, the United Kingdom alone produces 7000 doctors, and so, the sums quickly become enormous. In addition, there are nurses, pharmacists and allied health professionals—each of whom should receive the best possible initial and continuing education to help them achieve what everyone wants to achieve: a workforce that is educated to world-class standards.

However, to become world class is expensive, and it is always worthwhile to wonder whether you are getting value for money. So, are we getting value for money from the education of our health professionals? First, is the education of health professionals effective, and second, is it as cost-effective as it could be? The short answer to both these questions is that no one really knows. The first question on the effectiveness of medical education is perhaps the easier to answer. Medical educational research is still in its early years, but it has made progress, and we now know much more than we did about what constitutes effective medical education. For example, we know that the active participation of learners in

1

small groups is likely to be better than passive attendance at a lecture along with 200 other learners.[1] We know that assessment and exams should be practical, reliable and valid tests of applied knowledge, problem-solving skills and simulated behaviours rather than assessment of academic and seldom-applied knowledge.[2] We know that learning works best when it is practical and tied as closely as possible to the learner's everyday working life, and that learners are much more likely to change and improve their actual practice when they are educated in this way.[3] As our knowledge of the evidence base for effective learning has built up, many medical schools and postgraduate deaneries and providers of continuing professional education have stepped up to the mark and created new outcomes-based curricula, renovated their assessment methods and, in some cases, created workplace learning programmes. There is still a long way to go and we don't frankly know if medical education is as effective as it should be, but we do know that it is more effective than it was.

Many would say that the current state of medical education is healthy or at least that it is taking a penetrating look at its weaknesses, is seeing how best to address these and is developing a coherent vision of what medical education should be like. For example, most health professionals are now signed up to the need for medical education to be explicitly focussed on improving the knowledge, skills and behaviours of such professionals with the clear and ultimate outcome of improving patient care.[4] Most are signed up to the principle that, as health professionals work together in teams, they should learn together in teams and that the medical education community should pay more attention to integrated care and care pathways than it has in the past.[5] Finally, most agree that medical education provision should be based on the needs of individual clinicians and the needs of patients and communities for whom they are responsible.[6]

However, one big issue for medical education that has not really been addressed until now is cost effectiveness. That is where our real lack of knowledge comes to the fore. There have been very few systematic studies of the cost effectiveness of medical education, and so we don't really know the most cost-effective way to provide undergraduate, postgraduate or continuing medical education. Stated simply, we don't know the most cost-effective way of designing a curriculum, rolling it out or doing a final evaluation of it a few years later. Considering the cost of medical education, there is remarkably little known about its cost effectiveness. There is little known about how to calculate costs, about what constitutes costs or how to get maximal value for money. Up to now, there have been no books on this subject and precious few articles. Most of the articles that do exist are reviews that bemoan the lack of original research in this area. So, this is exciting territory. In the current international economic climate, cost effectiveness in medicine and in medical education is likely to come to the fore in the coming months and years. If providers and commissioners of medical education have limited budgets or budgets that have been cut back, then they are likely to want to know how best to spend their money. For these reasons, the problems and potential solutions outlined in the following chapters are likely to be timely and important.

The costs of *not* providing high-quality medical education should also be considered. The most important one is the human cost—medical error accounts for a massive amount of morbidity and mortality, and error is very common. Approximately 2% to 14% of medication orders contain an error, and this is just prescribing error.[7] Then, there is the financial cost to the health service in rehabilitating and caring for patients who have survived medical error as well as the costs to the economy in terms of lost productivity due to short- or long-term disability.[8] To close the circle, there are the costs of rehabilitating those health professionals whose standards are no longer up to scratch or may never have been up to scratch in the first place—possibly because of inadequate undergraduate or postgraduate education or inadequate continuing professional development. Remediating health professionals who need to improve their clinical or non-clinical skills can be a long and expensive process.

There will be those, like Drummond Rennie in the opening quote, who are sceptical of the value of cost-effectiveness analysis. His quote will find echoes in a health-professional audience who have slowly come to terms with the concept of analysis of the cost effectiveness of healthcare and know the difficulties of changing long-held opinions even with new and compelling evidence that these opinions are wrong. But, this is a policy of despair: like evidence-based medicine, evidence-based medical education must become the only show in town—regardless of how uncomfortable we may feel with the outcomes of new research or analyses into medical education and its cost effectiveness.

There will be still more critics who will bemoan the emergence of a new cadre of medical education cost-effectiveness analysts poring over direct and indirect costs of medical education resources. A famous and favourite quote for educationalists is that of Yeats–'education is not the filling of a pail but the lighting of a fire', which is a sentiment that will always sit uncomfortably with closely managed education that is held to strict fiscal account. However, the worldwide recession and economic winter facing many healthcare and health education budgets will mean that the cost of medical education will need to be measured and economies made when possible.

The questions that remain are how best to make such measurements and how and where to make economies—the following chapters will hopefully shed some light on how best to come up with answers to these questions. One question, though, can be answered at the start: high-quality and effective medical education is essential—we must never sacrifice this at the altar of cost.

REFERENCES

1. Mansouri M, Lockyer J. A meta-analysis of continuing medical education effectiveness. *J Contin Educ Health Prof.* 2007 Winter; **27**(1): 6–15.

2. Schuwirth LW, van der Vleuten CP. ABC of learning and teaching in medicine: written assessment. *BMJ.* 2003 Mar 22; **326**(7390): 643–5.
3. Evans K, Guile D, Harris J, *et al.* Putting knowledge to work: a new approach. *Nurse Educ Today.* 2010 Apr; **30**(3): 245–51.
4. Forsetlund L, Bjørndal A, Rashidian A, *et al.* Continuing education meetings and workshops: effects on professional practice and health care outcomes. *Cochrane Database Syst Rev.* 2009 Apr 15; **2**: CD003030.
5. Reeves S, Zwarenstein M, Goldman J, *et al.* The effectiveness of interprofessional education: key findings from a new systematic review. *J Interprof Care.* 2010 Feb 23; **24**(3): 230–41.
6. Miller BM, Moore DE Jr, Stead WW, *et al.* Beyond Flexner: a new model for continuous learning in the health professions. *Acad Med.* 2010 Feb; **85**(2): 266–72.
7. Lewis PJ, Dornan T, Taylor D, *et al.* Prevalence, incidence and nature of prescribing errors in hospital inpatients: a systematic review. *Drug Saf.* 2009; **32**(5): 379–89.
8. Ackroyd-Stolarz S, Guernsey JR, MacKinnon NJ, *et al.* Adverse events in older patients admitted to acute care: a preliminary cost description. *Healthc Manage Forum.* 2009 Autumn; **22**(3): 32–6.

CHAPTER 2

Cost-effective undergraduate medical education

Paul Finucane and Peter McCrorie

Some kids want to know why the teachers get paid when it's the kids who have to do all the work.

—*Milton Berle*

INTRODUCTION

We live in an era where consumers are better informed and demand a greater say in how their needs are addressed. Consumers are also increasingly cost conscious and demand value for their money, whether paying directly or indirectly through taxation. In response, governments are obliged to seek value when they spend tax revenue; this in turn impacts service providers. Those who deliver medical education are not immune from these societal and political pressures.

In the business world, a particular phenomenon has been the development of products that over time become more sophisticated and expensive, particularly when there is no competition. At some stage, the erstwhile monopoly provider is challenged by a competitor with a new and less sophisticated product that meets basic needs and that is delivered at reduced cost.[1] There are numerous examples (e.g., from the steel, aviation and retail grocery industries) where acceptable though unsophisticated cheaper products have displaced those that are both unnecessarily complex and more expensive. Stated simply, given the option of a cheaper alternative, consumers are often loath to pay for more costly and discretionary goods and services.

A central thesis in this chapter is that the educational processes that produce doctors have become increasingly expensive and are not well targeted at the needs of society. The scene is therefore ripe for the development of alternative educational processes that produce competent doctors but at reduced cost to society.

THE CURRENT STATE OF UNDERGRADUATE MEDICAL EDUCATION

Over the past 40 years in particular, medical education has been in a state of flux. Two important factors moulding its new shape are the changing face of medical practice and a better understanding of how students learn. Regarding the former, the stereotype of the solo and all-knowing medical practitioner whose competence was seldom questioned has been replaced by the team-worker with the ability to stay abreast of advances in medical knowledge and who is obliged to demonstrate continuing professional competence. In response, most medical schools now promote interprofessional education, embrace information technology and aim to produce graduates with lifelong learning skills. An increased emphasis on professionalism and social accountability translates into strategies to foster communication skills, ethical behaviour and the ability of graduates to recognise and respond to local and national health priorities.

During the last century, educational psychologists highlighted the limitations of rote learning and instead suggested that learners be stimulated to think, to confront their ignorance and to use this as a stimulus to acquire new knowledge. It was realised that knowledge is best gained in the context of how it is subsequently used and that adults learn most effectively when they control what and how they learn. Such insights have stimulated a move away from didactic and instructor-centred teaching towards more interactive and student-centred learning. Problem-based learning (PBL) is perhaps the most obvious exemplar of such trends. An appreciation of the impact of assessment strategies on student learning has led to the development of new ways of measuring the application of knowledge and the acquisition of clinical competence, rather than merely rewarding rote learning.

THE CHARACTERISTICS OF EFFECTIVE UNDERGRADUATE MEDICAL EDUCATION

The efficacy of any educational programme is best judged by the quality of its graduates. Although this statement is clearly a truism, such thoughts have only recently filtered through to the evaluation of medical school programmes whose quality has traditionally been measured by educational processes rather than outcomes. We now realise that outcome-based evaluations ensure that educational processes produce doctors who are fit for purpose.

Such thinking has prompted a number of national and international bodies (e.g., the UK's General Medical Council, the Association of American Medical Colleges, the

Scottish Deans' Medical Curriculum Group and the Tuning Educational Structures in Europe)[2,3] to define the essential competencies required of medical graduates. The widely acclaimed CanMEDs framework produced by the Royal College of Physicians and Surgeons of Canada in 1996 and updated in 2005[4] describes competencies in seven areas:

1 medical expert
2 communicator
3 collaborator
4 health advocate
5 manager
6 scholar and
7 professional.

As we focus on outcomes, we begin to critically evaluate the processes that generate them. For example, in ensuring that graduates are competent health advocates, a medical school needs to ensure that it provides the necessary resources and processes to produce this competence.

THE EXPLICIT COSTS OF AN UNDERGRADUATE MEDICAL PROGRAMME

Those costs that are immediately apparent can be categorised as infrastructure costs and human resource costs (*see* Box 2.1).

Box 2.1 The obvious costs of an undergraduate medical programme

Infrastructure costs
- New buildings and maintenance of existing buildings
- Laboratory facilities for teaching (e.g., anatomical dissection, physiological and microbiological experimentation, clinical and communication skills)
- Library
- Computer laboratories and videoconference facilities
- Laboratory facilities for research (e.g., 'wet' laboratories)
- Office accommodation
- Lighting, heating, cleaning and security

Human resource costs
- Salaries for faculty (full-time, part-time and sessional staff)
- Technical staff
- Administrative and support staff (both within the medical school and elsewhere within the university)

INFRASTRUCTURE COSTS

As most medical schools are long-established, the buildings in use tend to be part of the institution's fabric, so that only maintenance and service costs apply. Older buildings have higher maintenance costs, although expenses such as heating, lighting, cleaning and security apply to all. Many schools are responsible for several buildings, some on the university campus and others on the affiliated clinical sites. New schools and those with expanding student numbers are likely to incur additional capital costs for new buildings.

All schools need laboratories and these generally have high operational and maintenance costs. Traditionally, laboratories have been used for anatomical dissection and physiology and microbiology practicals. Although many schools have reduced or dispensed with such activities, there has been a compensatory need for alternative resources (e.g., sophisticated and expensive anatomical models, computer-generated images and ultrasound equipment to teach anatomy). Most schools now provide structured teaching in clinical and communication skills—these also require dedicated space and equipment.

All students need ready access to a well-stocked library, and senior students on clinical placements need to be able to access library facilities from remote clinical sites. Technological advances and the ready availability of laptop and hand-held computers are rapidly changing the ability of students to access information. The dramatic expansion of e-learning in recent years means that no medical school can now function without dedicated computer laboratories. Schools increasingly use videoconference facilities to engage with students, particularly if dispersed over several or remote clinical sites. Technology is also changing the face of student assessment processes, with increasing emphasis on online assessment.[5] Many schools therefore have invested and continue to invest heavily in information and communications technology.

The academic mission of most medical schools spans teaching and research. A discussion on the physical resources required for biomedical research is beyond the scope of this chapter. At any given time, these will be determined not only by the strategic plan of the school and host university but also by the ability of the institution to compete for research funding. However, almost all schools provide some core research infrastructure, some of which can be quite expensive, such as facilities required for animal experimentation.

Added to all of the above is the need for office space for staff on campus and at remote clinical sites.

HUMAN RESOURCE COSTS

By far, the greatest recurring items of expenditure for any medical school are the salaries of faculty, whether employed on a full-time, part-time or sessional basis on the host university campus or at affiliated clinical sites. The aggregated salaries of technical, administrative and other support staff are inevitably substantial. Some support staff are a direct cost to the medical school, whereas others, being employed centrally by the university, are an indirect cost.

THE HIDDEN COSTS OF AN UNDERGRADUATE MEDICAL PROGRAMME

Hidden costs arise from the failure or inability to accurately identify and cost all of the elements that contribute to a school's education and research agendas. To some extent, having robust business plans with accurate accounting mechanisms guards against this. However, some medical school activities are notoriously difficult to quantify and cost.

A classic example is the cost to clinical sites and to the healthcare system in having students on placement. Some argue that students introduce a 'drag factor' in slowing down ward rounds, outpatient clinics and other clinical activities. Similarly, students use hospital resources such as the libraries, tutorial rooms and even canteens and car parks, all at a cost to the clinical sites. The counter argument is that, if students are successfully integrated into clinical teams, they enhance productivity and can make a net contribution to patient care. Furthermore, the nurturing of students represents an investment in the future by the healthcare system. In some countries, the 'hidden' cost of clinical training is offset by a funding allocation to clinical sites. One example is the 'Service Increment for Teaching' (SIFT) fund that is provided to National Health Service (NHS)-funded institutions in the United Kingdom.

Some contend that research activity brings more hidden costs and that research grants seldom cover the requirements for time, space, equipment and consumables. School resources must therefore be diverted to fund research. Even accepting this argument, it is difficult to make such hidden costs more explicit because teaching and research activities are inextricably linked. Were it possible to measure the cost of biomedical research more explicitly, it is likely that most medical schools and their host universities would continue to cross-subsidise it, given the benefits and prestige associated with quality biomedical research.

Other medical school costs may be misclassified as 'hidden' whereas in reality, they are merely disregarded. This particularly arises in relation to episodic activities such as student assessment and course evaluation processes. These can be extremely demanding of time and energy, are a significant cost to all schools and should be quantifiable. It is also important to consider costs that are not necessarily borne by the school or university but are a cost to society. One example is the costly process of rigorous course evaluation undertaken by accrediting bodies.

COST-EFFECTIVE UNDERGRADUATE MEDICAL EDUCATION

Cost effectiveness is essentially a business management construct that seeks to generate a competitive edge by reducing production costs while maintaining a product of acceptable quality. As argued in the introduction to this chapter, the quality issue is central—a product that fails to meet consumer needs will fail no matter how low its price. While many people will bristle at the suggestion that medical education can be considered a business or that medical graduates can be regarded as a product, the fundamental question being posed is: 'How can medical schools continue to produce quality doctors but at less cost to society?'

HOW UNDERGRADUATE MEDICAL EDUCATION CAN BECOME MORE COST-EFFECTIVE

There are many conceptual frameworks to underpin strategies for making medical education more cost-effective. One such framework is the 'Six Sigma' (6σ) approach that has been adopted by many of the world's largest manufacturing industries over the past 20 years.[6] Despite having its detractors, 6σ has spawned its own industry in teaching people to understand and implement the process. Along with just about every other conceivable application, 6σ strategies are now being used in the delivery of healthcare and in medical education.

Stated simply, 6σ borrows from earlier approaches to quality improvement in devising strategies to reduce defects and variability in the quality of what is produced. As a secondary outcome, greater efficiency usually results in decreased production costs and greater profit. Using the 'DMAIC' acronym, the process has five steps:

1 *Define* the key desired outcomes in broad terms, together with the current processes of achieving them
2 *Measure* key aspects of the current process (i.e., collect data)
3 *Analyse* the data and determine cause-and-effect relationships
4 *Improve* the process by devising and implementing new strategies
5 *Control* to prevent the improvement being diluted or against a return to the status quo.

It is crucial that all those involved in the production process from the CEO to those working on an assembly line buy into the 6σ approach. To this end, a parallel management structure has been developed for 6σ with those involved being accorded the titles 'Executive Leaders', 'Champions', 'Master Black Belts', 'Black Belts' and 'Green Belts'. The first three named are those who generally identify the projects to be undertaken, while the Black Belts and Green Belts are responsible for their execution. With such titles come responsibility and an expectation that those who have signed up will contribute.

A related concept of 'lean thinking' also comes from industry. As the name suggests, this aims to reduce waste and inefficiency by eliminating unnecessarily complex and time-consuming practices and by directing resources to where they will yield the greatest return. Lean thinking has been allied to 6σ to produce 'Lean 6σ'—strategies to reduce costs while enhancing the quality of the product.

In applying the Lean 6σ approach (or indeed any comparable business management tool) to undergraduate medical education, the task is therefore to *define* what we wish to achieve through our educational processes, to *measure* the way in which we currently undertake this task, to *analyse* the data and so continue, using the DMAIC approach. Some might argue that their particular institution is already engaged in such processes—for example, that its annual curriculum conference provides an opportunity to reflect on and modify the existing educational processes. However, Lean 6σ differs in creating a culture that permeates the organisation, such that cost reduction and quality enhancement strategies are part and parcel of daily life.

We earlier discussed the emphasis on outcomes that now exists in medical education. This fits in neatly with approaches such as Lean 6σ. For example, it might prompt a medical school to revise its approach to the delivery of PBL, to anatomy teaching or to clinical training in paediatrics.

It follows from the above that, if operating in isolation, there is relatively little that an individual can do to improve cost-efficiency within an organisation. Rather, the individual must be part of an ongoing organisational effort to improve quality and to increase efficiency. That stated, an individual within an organisation can provide leadership and perhaps help to identify areas that are ripe for a DMAIC or similar approach.

POTENTIAL COST-EFFECTIVENESS STRATEGIES IN UNDERGRADUATE MEDICAL EDUCATION

In looking at cost-effectiveness strategies, the first step for an individual medical school is to identify the components of the programme on which to focus. Although these will largely be specific to the school in question, there are a number of strategies that might be considered by all schools.

- Reduce the duration of courses: Courses of six or more years' duration are now rare, the norm being five-year courses for high school entrants and four-year courses for graduate-entry students. However, two Canadian schools (McMaster University and the University of Calgary) produce quality graduates through highly intensive three-year programmes. Although shorter programmes are attractive to students, governments and society, the potential associated revenue loss makes them less attractive to universities.
- Reduce student attrition: Between 5% and 15% of medical school entrants withdraw or are excluded from courses before graduation, at significant cost to the students, their medical schools and to society. While a detailed discussion on strategies to reduce attrition rates is beyond the scope of this chapter, we now know that attrition rates are reduced by recruiting more mature and highly motivated students with a track record of achievement in third-level education. Clearly, the manner in which students are supported and mentored once on the programme also impacts attrition rates.

- Review approaches to teaching and learning: Although recent pedagogic innovations are geared towards improving the learning experience, they can also reduce costs. Examples include the greater emphasis on self-directed learning (or directed self-learning), e-learning and virtual patients.[7] The use of podcasts and other technologies avoids the need to repeat teaching sessions, while allowing students to access material when and where they choose. While embracing the new, the outmoded (and costly) educational practices should be discarded. For example, we believe that 'wet laboratory' practicals have no role in modern medical education.
- Promote collaboration: Within an institution, interprofessional education not only promotes teamwork but also reduces replication of teaching across disciplines. Inter-institutional collaboration can minimise replication in areas such as student selection, curriculum development, provision of teaching materials and resources and student assessment. National collaborations might usefully focus on the provision of a common exit examination for all graduates.[8] International collaborations are also gaining momentum, perhaps now stimulated by the ease of communication and information transfer.
- Re-evaluate manpower requirements: As already noted, most of a medical school's expenses relate to staff salaries, so that any debate on cost effectiveness has to focus on staff numbers and productivity. Many schools can no longer afford to employ large numbers of full-time faculty, some of whom make only modest contributions to teaching and research. Instead, they now rely more on part-time or sessional faculty to deliver specific elements of the curriculum (e.g., as PBL tutors, clinical skills tutors or guest external lecturers).
- Reconsider the role of academic departments: The increasing sub-specialisation of medicine has resulted in a proliferation of clinical departments and academic appointments in an ever-expanding range of disciplines. 'Successful' academic departments are characterised by their size and rapid growth rate. While they often attract significant grant funding and thus enrich schools and universities, society ultimately foots the bill. That stated, it is essential for all medical schools to have a critical mass of full-time senior academic staff to provide the 'glue' that holds the teaching and research programmes together, to provide leadership and to help portray the school's identity.
- Consider role substitution: Many of the traditional tasks of doctors are now undertaken just as effectively by other health professionals (e.g., physician assistants, clinical nurse specialists or anaesthetic practitioners) who require shorter periods of training and who are less expensive to employ. This trend is likely to increase over time. Although it will not impact directly on the cost effectiveness of medical education, it will have a significant impact on the cost of health-service delivery.
- Provide more focused and less generic medical education: Allied to the above is the fact that, currently, much core medical education is not particularly relevant to a graduate's eventual area of specialist practice. This raises many questions:

How much exposure to orthopaedic surgery, obstetrics and oncology is essential for a future child psychiatrist or dermatologist? Should less time be spent on studying the basic and clinical sciences that underpin the various aspects of general medical practice? If so, does this cause a 'dumbing down' in medical education? Perhaps the time is now ripe to re-evaluate the role of a doctor in the 21st century. There is a strong argument for providing only focused graduate-entry programmes of four-year or perhaps three-year duration, where the emphasis is on critical reasoning and on diagnostic and management conundrums. The more mundane aspects of healthcare delivery might be left to others.

CONCLUSIONS

If the discipline of medical education is to remain relevant, it needs to be dynamic and capable of responding to changing societal needs. Ideally, it should anticipate change and help to drive the change process. Considerations of cost effectiveness do not yet feature highly on the reform agenda in medical education; the inexorable rise of consumerism means that this is soon likely to change. One of the major new challenges for undergraduate medical educators is to reduce costs while producing competent medical graduates.

REFERENCES

1. Christensen CM. *The Innovator's Dilemma: when new technologies cause great firms to fail.* Boston, MA: Harvard Business School Press; 1997.
2. Scottish Deans' Medical Curriculum Group. The Scottish doctor – learning outcomes for the medical undergraduate in Scotland: a foundation for competent and reflective practitioners. *Med Teach.* 2002; **24**(2): 136–43.
3. Cumming AD, Ross MT. *The Tuning Project (medicine) – learning outcomes/competences for undergraduate medical education in Europe.* Edinburgh: The University of Edinburgh; 2008. Available at: www.tuning-medicine.com (accessed 9 November 2009).
4. Frank JR, editor. *The CanMEDS 2005 Physician Competency Framework. Better standards. Better physicians. Better care.* Ottawa: The Royal College of Physicians and Surgeons of Canada; 2005.
5. Dennick R, Wilinson S, Purcell N. On-line eAssessment: AMEE Guide No. 39. *Med Teach.* 2009; **31**(3): 192–206.
6. Pande P, Holpp L. *What is Six Sigma?* New York, NY: McGraw-Hill; 2001.
7. Ellaway RH, Poulton T, Smothers V, *et al.* Virtual patients come of age. *Med Teach.* 2009; **31**(8): 683–4.
8. McCrorie P, Boursicot KAM. Variations in medical school graduating examinations in the United Kingdom: are clinical competence standards comparable? *Med Teach.* 2009; **31**(3): 223–9.

CHAPTER 3

Cost-effective postgraduate medical education

Hemal Thakore

Good teachers are costly but bad teachers cost more.

—Bob Talbert

INTRODUCTION

The focus of this chapter is to answer the question of whether or not we are producing doctors who are effective or competent in relation to the cost of their training. Surprisingly, this question does not seem to have arisen very often in various medical education debates which have taken place around the world. However, in light of the current economic downturn, the question has even greater relevance. Historically, the medical profession tends to resist measures that limit or reduce postgraduate training, both in terms of finance and the time taken to achieve completion of training. However, the major reforms—initially in undergraduate medical education with the advent of the UK General Medical Council's 'Tomorrow's Doctors' report[1] and then the subsequent graduate training reforms with relatively recent inception of the UK Postgraduate Medical Education and Training Board—have begun to shine a light (albeit dimly) onto the area of cost effectiveness.[2] The beam has been somewhat sharpened with the onset of the new European Working Time Directive (EWTD) that effectively limits the number of hours that a doctor can spend at work every week. Finally, if we also throw into the mix the concept of evidence-based medicine (EBM) and the shift from what the profession thinks is right for training to what the patient and the taxpayer think is right, the situation is frankly in a state of flux.

WHAT IS EFFECTIVE POSTGRADUATE MEDICAL EDUCATION?

What are we looking for as the key outcome in cost-effective postgraduate medical education? To begin with, we must find out what constitutes *effective* postgraduate medical education. This question can generate a variety of answers depending on which community (professional, public or health service) is asked. Most groups, when asked what elements make up an effective postgraduate training programme, would come up with the following major components: curricula, examinations, experience, facilities, research, teachers and, of course, time.

Constructive use of time spent in quality training is important in answering the question of what is effective postgraduate medical education. In any analysis of cost effectiveness, both time and content of training will feature as being paramount in determining whether a programme delivers an effective product, namely an independent specialist. In respect to time, the medical profession and, in particular, the surgeons have stated that doctors in their speciality cannot meet the EWTD requirements and at the same time become competent as specialists. Combined, the 'New Deal'[3] and the Calman report[4] have succeeded in reducing the time available to train a surgeon from 13 years at over 100 hours a week to 8 years at 56 hours a week—a reduction by nearly two-thirds.[5] This was before the final reduction to a 48-hour working week by 2009 to comply with the directive.

Other professions have echoed these sentiments, and the crux of their argument lies in the fact that having a shift-working doctor doing only 48 hours a week, will not allow exposure to all of the correct case-mix balance that a trainee specialist requires to become an expert. Exposure to the correct case-mix is vital in providing an effective, quality education programme for trainees. However, proponents of the EWTD have often pointed out the fact that working longer hours makes a doctor less effective and less safe and that the tasks performed during the longer week were not focused exclusively on training but on other more administrative or basic clinical procedures (i.e., form filling and blood taking). Although some of the burden of these 'lesser tasks' might have been removed from junior doctors, it still falls on their shoulders to ensure that the patients get clinically managed on a daily basis. Shift patterns will also have to take account of case-mix, especially of acute and trauma cases, which can present in an erratic manner on a weekly basis.

The content of training programmes and, crucially, how the content is delivered, learnt and assessed are important determinants of cost effectiveness. Making sure that the working week focuses on quality training might not be easy to achieve. This is particularly important given the move towards the adoption and implementation of competency-based training programmes for most postgraduate medical education.[6] The development of the necessary knowledge, skills and attitudes for independent specialist practice is not time-limited in this model, and we may find that the time required to become competent may require adjustments to the traditional fixed-period training rotation concept. This is because a doctor is not considered fit for independent specialist practice until she or he has demonstrated competence of the programme objectives to a specified degree. This is unlike the traditional training models that were heavily based on the concept of experiential rotation-based learning combined with obtaining a diploma from their relevant postgraduate specialist college. Assessment of these diploma examinations was all too often by formal examination methods [e.g., written papers, multiple-choice questions (MCQs), objective structured clinical examinations (OSCEs)]. There is little emphasis on workplace-based assessment that focuses on performance in practice with feedback—an integral part of the ideal assessment process.

Nobody could argue that a key cost-effective measurement would be to ensure that the trainee is fit for purpose by assessment of her or his competency based on performance in practice.

In the competency framework, trainees constructively use their experience to develop expertise by reflecting on and further developing their performance in practice. In fact, the competency-based training model will require development of some of the other factors that were mentioned earlier, such as training programmes (curricula and examinations), teachers (trainers) and facilities (location and ancillary buildings and equipment). In the competency-based model, educational activities occur around a transparent educational framework that is domain-based with underlying learning objectives specified in terms of not just knowledge but also skills and attitudes. These objectives must then be blueprinted into a training curriculum in terms of what must be achieved, how it is to be achieved and how it is to be monitored and ultimately assessed.

Cost-effective training can only be delivered by appropriately resourced and developed training staff. Training and developing the teaching instinct in trainers, both medical and nonmedical, will be important in determining cost effectiveness. Without investment in faculty development in terms of both time and money, we cannot hope to deliver a quality programme that produces a competent specialist. Therefore, a key component in the successful adoption of competency-based training will be faculty development. More effort is and will be required in producing better-equipped trainers who are more suited to the task of guiding and assessing junior doctors on their training pathway. Faculty, specifically competency-based trainers, educational supervisors and the multiple different assessors (e.g., other nonmedical health professionals participating in 360-degree feedback) all need to be given training in how to implement the new curriculum. If domains outside of pure medical expertise are to be included in training programmes (e.g., management, leadership and professionalism), then trainers need to be trained in teaching and assessing these aspects as well. In fact, some of the trainers will not themselves have received any formal training in some of these other domains but may have picked up these skills as part of their professional practice over a number of years. This will have to be accounted for in the creation and implementation of faculty-development programmes.

As mentioned previously, competency-based curricula focus on the acquisition of the right sets of knowledge, skills and attitudes in each of the specialties, with regular review of progress by a multitude of methods, including examinations and interviews. Assessment, as always, will form a critical part of determining whether competency has been achieved. The move towards assessing performance in practice will require the adoption of novel assessment tools such as the assessed clinical encounter, direct observation of procedural skills, 360-degree feedback and case-based discussions. The continual evaluation of candidates during practice, using multiple tools along with input and feedback from multiple examiners (medical and nonmedical), will also help assess less-tangible qualities such as professionalism, which cannot be reliably assessed by a single tool on one or two separate occasions. Rather these skills will be assessed continually using multiple workplace-based methods with trainees given feedback to reflect on their progress.

In summary, effective postgraduate medical education produces a competent specialist by the correct utilisation of training time, training experience, trainee assessment, teaching curriculum, learning environment and teachers. All of these factors require constructive alignment into a successful postgraduate training framework in which the training objectives are aligned with the curriculum/learning environment and with the assessment, and in which the trainers are skilled in bringing out the best in the learning opportunities that occur during training.

WHAT ARE THE COSTS INVOLVED IN EFFECTIVE POSTGRADUATE MEDICAL EDUCATION?

Next, we turn to the costs involved in postgraduate medical education. Most of us can readily identify the obvious costs: trainee and trainer salaries, maintaining the postgraduate educational curricular and assessment framework, maintaining the teaching facilities and payment for postgraduate assessment, coursework and research. There are also additional, hidden costs involved in the process as well. In fact, some of these are the obvious costs, which are not paid for by anyone, but on which a significant part of the current system exists. Not all training time is paid for; trainees have and will always put in considerable additional hours acquiring skills that will not receive remuneration but that may still contribute to patient care. Trainers have historically given of their time freely in the educational betterment of their trainees. Given the competency-based model mentioned previously, the cost for postgraduate education and training will inevitably rise when expenses for developing and maintaining such programmes are factored into the equation. The cost of freeing up more consultants' time away from patient care into providing structured education and assessment activities with trainees is another financial outlay. This will be in addition to the cost of training consultants to train their trainees properly. To date, no cost analysis of the financial outlay for this training model has been performed.

Another hidden cost, while not strictly financial, is the cost to patients in terms of their care. What has the patient either lost or gained by the new training frameworks put in place? While we strive to maintain patient safety, does the new model of time-constrained and fiscally contained training place the patient and his or her care fairly and squarely in the centre of the training versus clinical service equation? In other words, will doctors spending less time on the wards result in patients gradually becoming mere commodities to be practiced upon to achieve expertise as quickly as possible? What will be the effect on the doctor–patient relationship? Perhaps, the new assessment models that aim to examine these so-called 'softer' skills will help give us future insight. However, this is a critical question and its determination will be central to the concept of effective postgraduate medical education in terms of the patient and the community. In particular, will the overall reduction in weekly training time imposed by the EWTD result in a raw deal for patients, relegating them to becoming a repository of signs and symptoms which must be checked-off on an outcomes curricular list? This is a real concern, particularly if outcomes-based training is misperceived and reduced to deliver the minimum training required to meet the programme objectives.

HOW DO WE PROVIDE COST-EFFECTIVE MEDICAL EDUCATION?

Having looked at the issues surrounding cost-effective postgraduate medical education, how do we actually go about providing it? If the answer was obvious, I don't think that this book would need to be written. However, as opaque as it might seem, there should be a way of providing the healthcare system with fully trained doctors at an appropriate cost.

To provide cost-effective postgraduate medical education, we need to ensure that we have identified the correct competencies not just in clinical expertise but in terms of knowledge, skills and attitudes. These competencies must be built into a training framework that prescribes how, when, where and at what level they are to be achieved. The assessment of these competencies must be a continual process, based predominantly in the workplace, with feedback on progress given to trainees. To achieve these steps, trainers need to undergo faculty development, and this will demand a cost in terms of finance and time spent away from direct patient care. Finally, we will need to move away from an exclusive time-limited model of training where completion is based on the numbers of years spent training to one where completion is judged on achieving competency to participate in practice as an independent specialist. Let us look at some of these points in more detail.

If we hope to provide cost-effective medical education, then surely the first step should be to create an appropriate training programme. As more specialities move towards a competency-based training model, we should be in a position to validate the cost effectiveness of this curricular approach. Having a transparent framework in terms of not just outcomes but also in terms of how, when, where and at what level it is assessed will provide opportunities to look at the cost of putting a trainee through the process. A danger here, however, might be that in implementing such frameworks, the health service and other relevant agencies may select components and educational strategies that focus on the delivery of a minimum-acceptable training standard, with inadequate resources provided for faculty development and also for adequate delivery of education that is not directly patient-care related (e.g., other nonmedical expert domains such as communication and management). The delivery of continual workplace-based assessment and feedback, in particular the time spent away from direct patient care, will have a significant cost implication that must be factored into the delivery of postgraduate training programmes.

Cost-effective medical education relies on being able to measure the expense of training a doctor against the quality of the finished product (i.e., the specialist) and to thereby determine whether the resources put into that training process have been justified. Therefore, being able to positively identify the correct outcomes for postgraduate medical education is critical to ensuring that doctors are fit for purpose at the completion of their training and would, of course, be central both to producing a quality product and to seeking maximal cost effectiveness. Traditional training programme outcomes have tended to focus on skills that demonstrate knowing and showing competence and not, as previously discussed, focusing on *unconscious competence*, in essence, the 'mastery' part. Developing systems that allow for the monitoring of this level of competence are vital in ensuring that doctors meet the requirements of their training at a level where they can be trusted as independent practitioners. To produce an inferior product would not be professionally acceptable and would be cost consuming in the long term by virtue of having to provide remediation and retraining to those who ultimately fail as independent practitioners.

In the final analysis, we must ask the question: do we create training programmes around a fixed time-limited framework or should we, as competency-based education tells us, allow the trainee adequate time to master the competencies required to become a specialist who will be able to meet the challenges of both today and tomorrow?

Objectives alone, without the proper learning environment, will not provide cost-effective medical education. Central to the acquisition of the appropriate knowledge, skills and attitudes in becoming an expert is the learning environment. Experience and reflection in practice is critical to becoming a specialist. The learning environment in this case is the hospital, general practice, laboratory or clinic where the trainee will spend a considerable amount of his or her training time. The learning environment should ideally be the workplace or at least replicate the actual practice environment in which the trainee will ultimately practice as an expert. This environment should also encourage the development of the nontechnical skills required by a potential specialist, especially the aspects of communication, ethics and professionalism. Leadership, management and teamwork are key skills that need to feature in this learning environment. Developing a multiprofessional training programme where core skills can be taught to the healthcare group, rather than each individual separately, would be at the core of developing a cost-effective educational pathway.

Simulation has a role to play in cost-effective postgraduate education. Why? Not everything can be learned on the ward or in the classroom. In particular, practical skills can be learnt first in a safe, simulated environment where patient safety is not at risk. Is it cost-effective? Well, this question is best answered by stating that the cost in setting up and maintaining these facilities is high. However, the benefit of allowing deliberate, focused practice in a virtual environment—particularly of difficult or high-risk clinical procedures and where supervision and feedback can be of a higher quality due to the nature of the technology and the ability to stop and start the simulation and reflect—should, in the long run, be cost-effective. A key point in developing these facilities is not to develop them in speciality isolation but rather to develop multi-professional simulation centres that can be used at the same time by different health professional groups working in teams.

In summary, to provide cost-effective postgraduate medical education, we need to ensure that we adopt a competency-based training framework and develop the teaching faculty who are to implement and assess it. Competency must be more than just knowledge recall and must include appropriate skills and attitudes, not just in the domain of clinical expertise but in multiple other domains. Continual workplace-based assessment with feedback to trainees will help to maximise cost-effective delivery by ensuring alignment between objectives and curriculum. It will also allow trainees to reflect on their ongoing development. To provide such a cost-effective training system would demand significant ongoing investment both in human and physical resources that, if developed properly, will ultimately pay dividends by the production of highly skilled specialists who place performance in practice at the heart of their ongoing professional development (*see* Table 3.1).

TABLE 3.1 Postgraduate medical education programme

Cost-effective	*Non-cost-effective*
Competencies for programme are identified in terms of knowledge, skills and attitudes.	Trainee will learn from time spent working in various rotations.
Competencies are not just focused on clinical expertise, but include other domains such as professionalism.	Training programme focuses on the acquisition of clinical expertise.
Framework for obtaining competencies is developed.	Training is predominantly rotation-based and focused on experiential learning.
Teaching faculty are trained to deliver curriculum and given dedicated time to teach.	Trainers train when they can and balance this with ongoing clinical care.
Assessment is continuous and based on performance in practice with feedback to trainees.	Formal assessments are taken at fixed time periods; not appropriately aligned with curriculum; provide no feedback.
Training is complete when trainee is considered competent.	Training is complete upon rotation completion and success at membership examination.

CONCLUSIONS

In summary, there is an imperative to make postgraduate medical education cost-effective. However, this can only be achieved if we know what we are producing and how much it currently costs to produce it. Neither of these questions has yet been answered. Whereas there are a myriad of new frameworks and structures in place for training doctors today, there is little evidence to demonstrate that these current strategies are effective in producing the specialists of tomorrow. Perhaps the move towards adoption of a competency-based model for postgraduate medical education will allow us greater transparency in determining not just outcomes but the associated costs in achieving those outcomes.

Postgraduate training and assessment must be aligned with learning objectives that cover appropriate knowledge, skills and attitudes. These also need to be properly costed. Critically, the curriculum must encompass the needs not only of the profession but also the expectations of the patient and the health system in which the doctor will function. Integration into the health-provision system will be of utmost importance and an increased focus on interprofessional education will be required, both as necessary educational and cost-effective measures.

If we are to produce competent, effective doctors at reasonable cost, then we should consider answering some of the questions posed in this chapter, namely, what is the best curriculum to develop future specialists, how can this curriculum be delivered and assessed and how can we support the deliverers of this process. Finally, we must not forget the patient in all of this. We need to ensure that cost-effective medical education places the patient firmly in the centre of the training equation. The patient must not be viewed as a commodity to learn from but as the touchstone for the development of a caring professional. True professionals are aware of their responsibilities not only to their profession but also to themselves and, most importantly, to their patients and the public as well.

REFERENCES

1. General Medical Council. *Tomorrow's Doctors*. London: GMC; 2003.
2. Neal D, Bruce L, MacPherson S. The role of the Postgraduate Medical Education and Training Board (PMETB). *Surgery (Oxford)*. 2008; **26**(10): 403–7.
3. National Health Service Medical Executive. *The New Deal: plan for action*. Leeds: NHSME; 1994.
4. Department of Health. *Hospital Doctors: training for the future*. London: DoH; 1993.
5. Bulstrode C, Holsgrove G. Education for educating surgeons. *BMJ*. 1996; **312** (7027):326–7.
6. Harden R. Outcome-based education: the future is today. *Med Teach*. 2007; **29**(7): 625–9.

CHAPTER 4

Cost-effective continuing professional development

John Sandars

The illiterate of the 21st century will not be those who cannot read and write, but those who cannot learn, unlearn, and relearn.

—*Alvin Toffler*

INTRODUCTION

All healthcare professionals need to keep their knowledge, skills and attitudes updated to ensure that they can provide high-quality healthcare. The pace of change in healthcare is swift, and there is colossal financial investment each year to provide the necessary training to keep up. In a world of increasing financial pressures, a wide range of providers are beginning to question the cost effectiveness of this training. Are providers getting value for money? This is an important question but not easily answered. The concept of cost effectiveness initially appears to be simple—it considers the costs required to provide a desired outcome. However, the associated issues are more complex. This chapter will discuss the difficulties that are inherent in the measurement of cost effectiveness for continuing professional development (CPD) and will highlight the problems of identifying the effectiveness of this form of education and how the associated costs can be calculated. Finally, the future of cost-effective CPD is discussed, and several practical approaches to overcome the identified difficulties are proposed.

WHAT IS CPD?

CPD is a process by which healthcare professionals keep constantly updated so that they can effectively respond to the demands that they face in their daily professional work.[1] Continuing medical education (CME) is only one aspect of CPD. First, CPD recognises that the updating is for all healthcare professionals rather than only doctors, and second, it highlights the importance of including a wide range of topics, including managerial and personal skills that are beyond the traditional clinical medical subjects. The provision of high-quality healthcare is complex and effective education requires a broad range of topics to be covered. The acquisition of new knowledge and skills is an essential aspect of CPD, but the opportunity to challenge and redefine attitudes is also important, especially when healthcare professionals are increasingly making ethical and moral decisions about the care that they provide.

There are a wide variety of approaches that are used to provide CPD. Formal methods include courses, lectures, study days and workshops. The range of informal approaches is wider, from audit to reflecting on day-to-day practice.

WHAT IS EFFECTIVE CPD?

Effectiveness is a nebulous concept that implies that it is possible to measure the effect of a particular intervention. A widely used approach to evaluate any educational intervention considers its impact at several levels: reaction, learning, behaviour and results.[2] Reaction is the level of satisfaction that participants feel about the educational intervention and is the most commonly used method, such as the ubiquitous evaluation questionnaire that appears at the end of most CPD events. It is important to meet the expectations of users, but these findings can hardly justify the expenditure without considering the actual learning that has occurred for the professional. Evaluating the learning is usually a self-perception of change in knowledge, skills or attitudes. There is sometimes a measurement of knowledge, such as by a multiple-choice test, but rarely are changes in skills or attitudes tested. It is important to know whether an educational programme actually changes the way the professionals behave—do they do things differently? The ultimate endeavour of healthcare professionals is to improve the quality of care that they provide, and there is interest in whether improved results can be achieved by the education.

A recent review of 26 systematic reviews of the effects of CME on improving physician clinical care and patient health identified that interactive techniques were the most effective at simultaneously changing physician care and patient outcomes.[3] These techniques included audit with feedback, academic detailing and reminders. Clinical practice guidelines and opinion leaders were less effective. Didactic presentations and distributing printed information only had little beneficial effect in changing physician practice. A more detailed look at the studies that were included in the various reviews highlights that the topics were not chosen by individual physicians or patients but were selected by healthcare providers as part of quality-improvement initiatives. This raises important issues concerning whose perspective is used to define effectiveness.

The provision of healthcare and the effectiveness of an educational intervention have a variety of perspectives. It is important that these perspectives are considered since they will influence both the nature and time frame of the educational intervention and the expected impact. Typically, these factors will also determine the amount of resources, including funding, allocated to the training. The provision of CPD and education by professional bodies and commercial organisations are usually based on a complex mix of these perspectives.

Governments and policy makers will identify healthcare issues that they consider to be a priority and, subsequently, they will provide CPD and training, and also substantial funding, in an attempt to change the behaviour of healthcare professionals. The focus of education is usually specific, such as reducing smoking or increasing early detection of cancer, and it often involves several approaches. Effectiveness will be defined by an improvement in the health of the population; since this may take many years, it is usually defined by other indicators, such as referral rates which can be more easily measured. Recently, there has been increasing interest in using outcome measures that have been defined by patients, such as quality of life, but educational interventions to address these aspects are rarely performed.

Pharmaceutical companies have traditionally ploughed enormous sums of money to change physician behaviour through CPD, and these educational interventions are also likely to have a narrow focus using multiple approaches. Effectiveness will be mainly defined by the increased prescribing of particular products although an important aspect is improved quality of care and patient outcomes. Prescribing patterns can be easily measured.

Individual healthcare professionals regularly identify personal learning needs during their daily professional practice. These learning needs are wide, from clinical and managerial aspects of practice to dealing with ethical dilemmas. Meeting these needs is complex since they will not necessarily match the CPD being offered by governments, policy makers and pharmaceutical companies. Professionals will often informally seek information, opinion and support from colleagues. There is usually little external funding and provision available for formal education in these areas; rather, physicians meet over a cup of coffee. There may be no easily measured outcome, either short or long term, and the effectiveness of any educational intervention may only become apparent during professional practice, such as increased empathy or shared decision making. Simple measures, such as patient satisfaction scores on a questionnaire, hardly do justice to these key aspects of professional practice.

Commercial organisations and professional bodies offer a large amount of CPD. This is usually a mix of the earlier approaches, and the exact mix will depend on the main source of funding. There is supportive funding by governments, policy makers and pharmaceutical companies, but individual healthcare professionals can contribute. The effectiveness of most of these educational interventions appears to be rarely measured, and it is unusual for the results to be published in the public domain.

In summary, measuring effectiveness initially appears simple, but the reality is that what can be measured may not accurately reflect the essential aspects of professional practice.

WHAT ARE THE COSTS OF CPD?

Costs are incurred in the development, delivery and evaluation of any educational intervention. These costs can be categorised as direct and indirect costs. The full cost of education is the sum of both direct and indirect costs, but there may be additional intangible costs that have no financial implications, such as increased stress and inconvenience to learners who have to attend weekend courses and have to arrange childcare with their partners.

Direct costs are all those expenses related specifically to the provision of CPD and the educational intervention. These costs should include the wages and associated expenses of both the providers and the learners, including insurance and pension contributions, office space and clerical support. The costs of preparing, delivering and evaluating the intervention also need to be considered.

Indirect costs are those expenses that are not specifically related to the provision of CPD and the educational intervention but are necessary for the organisation to function, such as utilities, payroll and administrative services, wear and tear, rent and depreciation. Although these costs are less visible, they can be substantial.

Within both direct and indirect costs, there may be hidden costs that are not readily apparent, such as the provision of locum cover whilst learners are attending education or funding for the intervention by a research grant or charitable donation. Many CPD and education interventions will be provided by large organisations, such as universities, the National Health Service and pharmaceutical companies, where education is the responsibility of a small department and staff members have other jobs. This can lead to major difficulties in providing accurate estimates of costs. The use of 'off-the-shelf' educational interventions may appear to have a defined cost but closer inspection may identify hidden costs associated with the development.

In summary, measuring the costs associated with CPD is often difficult and may not accurately reflect the true costs associated with an educational intervention.

WHAT IS COST-EFFECTIVE CPD?

The main reason for considering the cost effectiveness of any educational intervention is to justify the cost of the education in view of the identified benefits, especially when the costs are perceived to be too high or the benefits produced are less than intended. The expected benefits need to be clearly identified, such as an increased knowledge score or improved patient care, so that the costs associated with achieving the particular outcome can be measured.

A critical review in 2002 of the cost effectiveness of CPD in healthcare identified only nine studies that included an economic analysis of an educational intervention.[4] The authors noted that the methodology of all of the studies was poor, with a lack of a uniform method of costing and analysis. The studies had been performed in a wide variety of contexts and did not measure the effect on patient care. Only one study considered multidisciplinary care and most studies were based in primary care. An important reason for considering the cost effectiveness of any educational intervention is to compare interventions to see whether one intervention produces an identical outcome for a lower cost. This requires a randomised controlled trial but none were identified in the review. The educational interventions were mainly related to providing education to increase screening for various conditions, with a smaller number providing structured education to treat mental health issues or prescribing.

A systematic review of studies reporting on the cost effectiveness of a variety of interventions to control the emergence of antimicrobial resistance identified 21 studies, with only six studies related to an educational intervention.[5] The overall conclusion was that there was an absence of good evidence concerning what was cost-effective and that the methodology was poor.

There have been a few studies since 2002 that have used randomised controlled trials to identify the cost effectiveness of CPD on patient-care outcomes. A study of prescribing in primary care compared a multicomponent intervention to promote the use of guidelines (including educational outreach visits, audit and feedback and computerised reminders) to a control group who received only passive dissemination of guidelines.[6] They found that the cost of promoting the guidelines was greater than the savings achieved during the course of their study, which lasted 1 year. However, their calculations show that after 2 years the money saved would have exceeded the costs. After that, the savings would increase every year. A recent study assessed the cost effectiveness of providing practical education to general practitioners in the management of acute shoulder problems.[7] An important aspect of this study was that it measured the impact on patient care using quality-adjusted life years (QALYs) and compared the cost of education with no training. The authors concluded that education was cost-effective.

In summary, it is rare for studies to measure the cost effectiveness of CPD and educational interventions and extremely rare to measure the impact on patient-care outcomes. Overall, the methodology of cost-effectiveness studies is poor.

WHAT IS THE FUTURE FOR COST-EFFECTIVE CPD?

The present economic situation has made everyone consider the financial implications of their activities, and the provision of CPD is no different. Education budgets are often the first to be reduced in times of financial stringency; yet, this is a false economy since education has the potential to ensure that cost-effective care is provided. The imperative is to justify CPD and educational interventions using cost-effectiveness arguments rather than relying on persuasion, which is often based on little more than assumptions.

The first step is for providers to recognise that identifying the relative cost effectiveness of different educational interventions is essential to inform policy and commercial decisions. This should allow appropriate funding of high-quality medical education research to be established. A recent review of experimental research in medical education noted that few medical education researchers used rigorous methods for conducting and reporting their investigations.[8] Important limiting aspects identified in the review were the complex nature of many educational interventions combined with a poor description of the intervention, the lack of important and useful behavioural or patient outcome measures, the lack of long-term follow-up to evaluate impact and the lack of comparison to no educational intervention. Many studies are performed in circumstances that offer poor generalisation to other settings, such as offering inducement payments to participate in the study. High-quality medical education research is essential and should be designed to answer specific problems of interest to providers, such as what benefits or outcomes are expected from the educational intervention and what alternative interventions should be compared and in what settings.

High-quality cost-effectiveness studies require careful identification of the direct and indirect costs that are associated with the educational intervention and also the comparison group. Costs can vary widely between different settings and times—it is essential to report the quantities of the various resources as well as their identified costs. Accurate identification of costs can be difficult and an estimate is often made that is based on assumptions. In such cases, it is essential to clearly describe the process of calculating the costs.

Medical education researchers will need to collaboratively work with economists to ensure that their research will be responsive to the needs of the economists. Cost-effectiveness studies in medical education are rare, and my experience is that economists who are interested in this subject are a very rare breed. The approach used by economists will be unfamiliar to most medical education researchers, and their use of mathematical modelling is likely to be totally alien.[9]

The presentation of the results of cost-effectiveness studies will need to be easily understood by policy makers and providers. The wider world of evaluation of educational interventions in commercial sectors uses several measures that are both unfamiliar and challenging to CPD. The impact of educational interventions is often presented as return on investment (ROI), which is the rate at which education returns what was financially invested. The direct and indirect costs are calculated to identify the total cost of the education. The effects of the education on the outcomes before and after the education are identified. The usefulness of ROI is that it provides a clear indication of the benefit of an educational intervention and is easily understood. However, baseline data on outcomes has to be collected, and outcomes have to be quantified in monetary terms. A more radical approach is to consider 'bottom line' evaluations that try to determine the value added from the education of each participant.

It is essential to curb the enthusiasm for economic evaluation of CPD by consideration of its major limitations. It may be both impractical and impossible to identify the true cost of CPD. The desire to improve clinical outcomes initially appears attractive, but there may be substantial hidden incremental costs that are associated with change in clinical behaviour and care. These costs are associated with the potential necessity to allocate more resources to the area of care: for example, increased compliance with guidelines on hypertension is likely to result in improved control of blood pressure, but there will be raised costs associated with the increased use of prescribed medications. Many clinical interventions also take several years to take their full effect, and it is essential to have education studies that have sufficiently long follow-up to identify the desired benefit.

An important consideration for any cost-effectiveness study is that not all benefits can be easily measured in monetary terms, and this is a particularly thorny issue for the cost-effectiveness evaluation of CPD. 'Professionalism' lies at the heart of professional practice, and there is no easy way to objectively measure this elusive concept.[10] Educational interventions to develop professional behaviours are essential for a lifetime of professional practice, and there is increasing evidence that improved doctor–patient relationships can improve clinical care, such as increased adherence to treatments. A challenge for practitioners and medical education researchers is to provide a cost-effectiveness evidence base for complex educational interventions, such as Balint groups or practice-based discussion groups.

CONCLUSIONS

It appears inevitable that some form of economic evaluation of the cost effectiveness of CPD will be requested by providers in the present, and foreseeable, economic climate. Measuring the cost effectiveness of CPD will be a major challenge since identifying the true costs of educational interventions and deciding on the appropriate expected benefits that are relevant to all stakeholders is not easy. It is possible that many healthcare professionals will vehemently refuse to consider issues around cost effectiveness in CPD, but this response is at their peril. All providers and regulators of CPD likely want evidence that education is value for money and that time on CPD activities can produce tangible changes in professional behaviours and ultimately improved clinical care. Now is the time to begin a response to this challenge and enter constructive dialogue on how CPD can be meaningfully evaluated.

REFERENCES

1. Peck C, McCall M, McLaren B, *et al.* Continuing medical education and continuing professional development: international comparisons. *BMJ.* 2000; **320**(7232): 432–5.

2. Kirkpatrick DL. *Evaluating Training Programs: the four levels.* 2nd ed. San Francisco, CA: Berrett-Koehler; 1998.
3. Bloom BS. Effects of continuing medical education on improving physician clinical care and patient health: a review of systematic reviews. *Int J Technol Assess Health Care.* 2005; **21**(3): 380–5.
4. Brown CA, Belfield CR, Field SJ. Cost effectiveness of continuing professional development in health care: a critical review of the evidence. BMJ. 2002 Mar 16; **324**(7338): 652–5.
5. Wilton P, Smith R, Coast J, *et al.* Strategies to contain the emergence of antimicrobial resistance: a systematic review of effectiveness and cost-effectiveness. *J Health Serv Res Policy.* 2002; **7**(2): 111–17.
6. Fretheim A, Aaserud M, Oxman AD. Rational prescribing in primary care (RaPP): economic evaluation of an intervention to improve professional practice. *PLoS Med.* 2006; **3**(6): e216.
7. McKenna C, Bojke L, Manca A, *et al.* Shoulder acute pain in primary health care: is retraining GPs effective? The SAPPHIRE randomized trial: a cost-effectiveness analysis. *Rheumatology (Oxford).* 2009; **48**(5): 558–63.
8. Ratanawongsa N, Thomas PA, Marinopoulos SS, *et al.* The reported validity and reliability of methods for evaluating continuing medical education: a systematic review. *Acad Med.* 2008; **83**(3): 274–83.
9. Gandjour A, Lauterbach KW. How much does it cost to change the behavior of health professionals? A mathematical model and an application to academic detailing. *Med Decis Making.* 2005; **25**(3): 341–7.
10. Stern DL. *Measuring Medical Professionalism.* New York, NY: Oxford University Press; 2006.

CHAPTER 5

Cost effectiveness in interprofessional education

Debra Nestel, Brett Williams and Elmer Villanueva

A teacher was asked to fill out a special questionnaire for the state. One question said 'Give two reasons for entering the teaching profession.' The teacher wrote 'July and August'.

—*Milton Berle*

INTRODUCTION

This chapter addresses cost effectiveness in interprofessional education (IPE). IPE occurs when 'members of more than one health and/or social care profession learn interactively together, for the explicit purpose of improving interprofessional collaboration (IPC) and/or the health/well-being of patients/clients'.[1] IPC describes the clinical application of IPE, the 'process in which different professional groups work together to positively impact healthcare'.[2] Hammick et al.[3] identify basic competencies for being an interprofessional practitioner. Knowledge-based competencies include understanding the roles and working contexts of other practitioners as well as the principles of effective teamwork. Skills competencies include applying relevant knowledge, in particular, effective verbal and written communications with colleagues from other professions and settings and the routine practice of identifying when collaboration is helpful. Finally, attitude competencies detail respect of others' views, values and ideas and the concept of IPE collaboration.

We use the term profession-specific to describe professions learning independently. We outline the current state of IPE, describe what constitutes effective IPE, identify obvious and hidden costs and then consider cost effectiveness. We draw on our experiences in Australia and the United Kingdom.

WHAT IS THE CURRENT STATE OF IPE?

The origins of IPE provide insight into its current state. IPE was first reported in primary care where multiple professions worked together to manage patients and/or clients.[4] IPE was practice-based and the realm of qualified medical and social professionals. Drivers to the expansion of IPE have been many and varied. At the level of service delivery, these include high-profile media reports of poorly integrated health and social care[5,6] and changes in the organisation of healthcare,[7,8,9] specifically, a shift from individual to team-based care, the patient safety movement, increasing specialisation within professions and the emergence of new health professional roles. At the level of education provision, early initiatives at the undergraduate level were in part driven by the potential to pool resources and economise delivery of undergraduate education.[10] More recently, contextualisation and alignment of health and social curricula with real clinical practice have created a platform for IPE.

The volume and content of peer-reviewed publications is one way of monitoring trends, despite the limitations of such an approach. A search of English language abstracts in Ovid MEDLINE using the term 'interprofessional education' shows a threefold increase in publications over the past two decades. IPE has penetrated undergraduate and continuing professional education and is reported in primary, secondary and tertiary care. There are specialist IPE postgraduate courses, professional associations, networks and conferences.[11,12,13] IPE has been shown to change learners' attitudes towards one another's profession, improve knowledge of IPC, enhance collaborative behaviour and improve the delivery of patient care.[14,15,16,17] A Cochrane Review of IPE found just six studies meeting inclusion criteria; four showed positive outcomes whereas two showed no changes.[18] Positive outcomes included development of an emergency department culture and increased patient satisfaction, more collaborative team behaviours and reduction of clinical error rates for emergency department teams, improved management of care delivered to domestic violence victims and increased mental health practitioner competencies related to the delivery of patient care.[19]

A second way of monitoring trends is to situate IPE in the context of the current discourse driving the promotion of its adoption (often with vigour not in proportion to its supporting evidence). Government reports in Australia and the United Kingdom detail current and anticipated future shortfalls in the health workforce due to social, political and economic pressures as well as the increasing complexity of the healthcare system. IPE is consistently proposed as just one solution to deal with shortfalls,[20] offering a workforce that is skilled, responsive and collaborative. Proponents of IPE argue that it is more likely than profession-specific approaches to produce a multi-skilled and collaborative healthcare workforce able to practice within, and across, a range of health and social environments.

WHAT CONSTITUTES EFFECTIVE IPE?

It is worth considering what effective can mean in this context. In any educational intervention, the impact (effectiveness) can be measured in different ways.

Kirkpatrick originally proposed four levels to evaluate the impact of educational interventions in vocational training.[21] Barr *et al.* modified and contextualised these levels for healthcare.[22] At Level 1, evaluation consists of participants' reaction to the programme (e.g., satisfaction with learning methods). Level 2 measures modification to attitudes, perceptions, knowledge and/or skills, whereas Level 3 evaluates the transfer of learning to the workplace. Level 4 identifies changes to organisational practice based on the educational intervention, and Level 5 measures changes to the patient/client.

Ideally, effective IPE would demonstrate changes at all levels. Most reported studies in IPE address Levels 1 and 2. Some studies evaluate impact at Level 3. For IPE in undergraduate education, it is not really feasible to demonstrate changes at Levels 4 and 5 since students are often ancillary to service delivery. IPE that is effective at Levels 4 and 5 is characterised by being practice-based, responding to a specific challenge, including dedicated study time with facilitated learning activities, contributions from experts, role-play, trigger videoclips, written action plans, newsletter updates and supervised clinical practice with feedback.

Profession-specific approaches to education mean that professions have limited opportunities to learn about one another. Effective IPE provides opportunities for students to gain insight into the contributions each profession makes to health and social care and similarities and differences in roles and responsibilities.

WHAT ARE THE OBVIOUS COSTS?

Although we propose that costs can be separated into 'obvious' and 'hidden', in IPE, costs are more complex than in profession-specific education. We consider obvious costs to be those directly associated with implementing an IPE activity, whereas hidden costs are those that surround the delivery. Of course, this definition has limitations. It is beyond the scope of this chapter to thoroughly explore all IPE activity costs. Therefore, we focus on those associated with traditional educational programmes but acknowledge that IPE may develop its own methodologies. Obvious costs of IPE include all the elements of educational programme implementation (i.e., a broad range of human and physical resources). Human resources include faculty to teach and administrators to manage the programme. Physical resources may include educational materials and spaces.

IPE most often occurs in face-to-face sessions. There are few examples of distant or self-directed IPE. Simulation-based methods play an important and increasing role. Educational methods vary, with discussion and experiential activities widely reported.

Costing becomes more complex depending on whether IPE is offered at undergraduate or postgraduate levels, in university or other educational institutions. Dedicated learning spaces are obviously part of the fabric of such institutions. However, specialised methods may require specialised facilities such as simulation centres, observation rooms, audiovisual and other 'record and review' infrastructure. If IPE is delivered through health service organisations, then learning spaces may be scarce. In educational institutions, there are likely to be issues of scheduling teachers, students and administrators to IPE who are from different programmes, schools, departments and faculties.

Allocation of costs across the institution requires careful consideration. In health services, any removal of staff from patient care has obvious costs. Although IPE activities are often workplace-based, implementation is likely to slow service delivery. Budgetary models within individual health services will determine the extent to which internal negotiation over costs is required.

IPE may include assessment and evaluation. The nature and amount will vary. Given that the goal of most IPE is improved collaborative practice, valid assessments are likely to be skills-based. Traditional skills assessments are labour-intensive, requiring observations by expert practitioners. Assessments usually address individual performance, but a basic principle of IPE is effective teamwork. Team-based assessments may be more valuable but require further validation to be fair, transparent and reliable.

IPE in rural and remote locations is also an important cost consideration. There is sometimes an intensified need for IPE in these locations because of limited breadth of skill in the workforce. Greater 'role sharing' may occur compared with urban areas where a wider range of professional disciplines coexist. Taking rural and remote clinicians out of service for training may be more costly than in urban areas depending on whether IPE is delivered in situ or at a central site.

WHAT ARE THE HIDDEN COSTS?

Although IPE has been reported in the literature for more than 20 years, in many countries, IPE is not mainstream. Rather, IPE at the undergraduate level is more likely to form a small part of a profession-specific curriculum. Therefore, there will be hidden costs in the development of curricula that would serve the needs of all those they are designed to benefit. These costs could be considered as 'one-off', but as in all curricula, especially new ones, they are dynamic and will require periodic review.

A significant development cost will be associated with identifying content and educational methods for IPE. Although such tasks have been undertaken and reported in the literature,[23] it is not uncommon for curriculum developers to 'reinvent the wheel'. However, there may be advantages with this approach by achieving higher levels of ownership and engagement. Whatever the case, curricula usually require contextualisation, reflecting the local health service, professional disciplines involved and education expertise.

Topics identified by teachers to be shared across several professional programmes included psychology, sociology, ethics, law, research methods, management, economics of health and social care, health promotion, study skills, quality issues, structural problems and computing skills.[24] There are challenges associated with teaching shared or generic topics or skills since different professions require different levels of understanding and competence. Is the topic taught to the lowest common denominator? For example, although client–clinician interactions will mostly be based on partnership or cooperative client-centred models, the goals of interaction with clients vary between professional groups. Further, some professions spend much more time in direct contact with clients, whereas for others, it is intermittent. Although client–clinician communication is generic, it is also highly specialised. Decision-making about how to support shared profession-specific or generic topics or skills will therefore be complex.

The effort involved in co-ordinating representatives across professions is potentially great. This is even before the work of curriculum development has commenced, which brings with it challenges of professional ownership. Champions from professional groups may be perceived to be driving their own agenda. The medical profession has traditionally been slower than others to join IPE at the undergraduate level although it has led initiatives in primary care. Already crowded curricula may reduce enthusiasm for additional content and time.

Of course, in sharing curriculum content and those who deliver it, there may be savings. However, these may be offset by the costs of co-ordinating. By definition, IPE involves multiple professions, so this may increase the number of teachers required. We need insight into whether professional representation at faculty level is required to ensure effectiveness. That is, do all professionals who are learning with and from each other need teacher representation?

Other hidden costs are associated with the evaluation of IPE activities. Several authors recommend robust evaluation strategies in an effort to measure the impact.[25,26] Such evaluations are expensive. Programme evaluation expertise may not reside within the faculty and so may have to be outsourced.

There are likely to be additional costs where health- and social-care professionals are not educated within one institution. In institutions where multiple professional groups are undergoing training, they may not be on the same campus or clinical site, so bringing students and faculty together will increase costs. There will also be costs associated with the upskilling of faculty to deliver IPE.

Finally, there is the issue of IPE timing. Most professional licensing and registration bodies acknowledge that understanding the roles of different professional groups with whom the clinician works is important. Therefore, it is fairly safe to assume that IPE will begin in undergraduate education, but at what point and for how long? The extent to which professional associations are committed to IPE as part of their registration or revalidation varies. There will be costs for educational institutions in meeting accreditation or similar processes of professional associations.

WHAT IS COST-EFFECTIVE IPE?

Once a proper determination has been made about the most meaningful outcomes and costs arising from IPE activities, it becomes a simple matter to consider the relative cost effectiveness of IPE compared with other educational activities. The general concepts of cost effectiveness in education as discussed previously hold true for IPE. However, some regard must be made to points particularly relevant to IPE activities.

The main reason for the lack of adequate cost-effectiveness information relating to an IPE activity is the lack of adequate information about costs, outcomes or both. Average cost effectiveness is a function of two pieces of information expressed as a ratio:

$$\text{Average cost-effectiveness ratio (ACER)} = \frac{\text{cost of an IPE activity}}{\text{effectiveness of an IPE activity}}.$$

Since the ACER can contain no more information than the lesser of its components, it is sensitive to any deficiencies in the means by which information about costs or outcomes is collected. At the most extreme case, the absence of information means that the ACER is unable to be computed. Even if information about the costs or outcomes of an activity is present, it may be of poor quality because of problems with study design, internal validity, bias, imprecision, surrogacy of the end points or a host of other issues.

There is no cost-effectiveness 'threshold'. That is, there is no point above or below which an IPE activity can be said to have attained or failed to attain cost effectiveness. One can estimate ACERs with relative ease. However, their proper interpretation and the value placed on their levels require the consideration of external information. For instance, say a researcher claims that the ACER of an IPE activity around colorectal cancer screening via faecal occult blood testing is estimated to be $32 000 per case detected. The value of this statement (Is $32 000 too high? Is it too low? Is it cost-effective in the absolute?) depends on external factors such as competing resource priorities, funding constraints, the effectiveness of downstream interventions and others.

When comparing between or among IPE activities, incremental cost-effectiveness ratios (ICERs) are preferred over comparisons of ACERs. The difference between ICERs and ACERs is evident in the formula for the former:

$$ICER = \frac{\text{cost of activity A} - \text{cost of activity B}}{\text{outcome of activity A} - \text{outcome of activity B}}.$$

ACERs estimate the cost effectiveness of an IPE activity against one with no activity at all, whereas ICERs estimate the cost effectiveness of an IPE activity against the next best alternative activity (ACER = ICER if the next best alternative is an activity with no cost and no effect). For example, IPE activity A designed to improve Pap smear attendance is rolled out nationally at a cost of $570 000 and results in 33.3 quality-adjusted life-years (QALYs) saved (ACER = $17 117 per QALY). Activity B (a modification of A) costs $120 000 less and results in 32.8 QALYs saved (ACER = $13 719 per QALY). However, the incremental cost-effectiveness ratio of activity A compared with activity B is $120 000/0.5 = $240 000 per QALY. A decision to adopt activity B in place of activity A based on the former's lower ACER will be extremely costly from the standpoint of the incremental effect.

When comparing between or among activities, there may emerge a situation in which one activity is both more effective and less costly than another. In such a case, the first activity is said to dominate the second, and the ICERs need not be calculated.

Finally, cost-effectiveness analyses are necessary, but not sufficient, for making decisions about the relative merits of IPE alternatives. Such analyses do not provide guidance about the ethical, social or political dimensions of allocating limited resources in the face of competing demands. In addition, adopting activities found to have acceptable ICERs will sometimes increase total costs (while maximising outcomes). Thus, any expectation by decision-makers that resource savings will result is not guaranteed.

At present, the lack of information relating to the costs or outcomes of IPE activities prevents the comparative assessment of different activities. Concerted effort should be brought to bear by researchers working in IPE to build the necessary components to conduct cost-effectiveness analysis. In this regard, improving the state of the quality and measurement of outcomes arising from IPE activities is probably a more difficult task compared with the improvements necessary in cost information. By using rigorous evaluation methodologies embedded in IPE activities, we can begin to gather evidence of patient-relevant outcomes (such as health-related quality of life) rather than surrogates of uncertain import (such as changes in test scores or attitudinal variations).

Consider the following scenario: a new dermatologic cream is released in the market that promises to improve a patient's self-reported results on the pSoriasis Knowledge IN Canada (SKIN) questionnaire. There is no information about its effect on a patient's quality of life or clinical remission rates. Would such a drug be approved for use? Why, then, do we allow similarly poor evaluations of the effectiveness of IPE activities to proliferate?

The following provides one such example based on an IPE activity, comparing delivery of care in an interprofessional training unit with a conventional ward for patients undergoing hip and knee procedures. The authors report a lower cost in the interprofessional training unit.[27]

CASE STUDY

Hansen, Jacobsen and Larsen recently attempted to estimate the cost effectiveness of treating patients undergoing management and rehabilitation for primary hip and knee replacement procedures in an interprofessional training unit or a conventional ward.[28] The interprofessional training unit was established 2 years earlier as a space for the supervised training of medical, nursing, occupational therapy and physiotherapy students in the collaborative management of patients with a focus on the optimisation of continuity of care.

All patients scheduled to undergo total hip or knee arthroplasty between September and December 2006 at a regional hospital in Denmark were randomly allocated to either the interprofessional training unit or conventional ward. Average daily costs in both wards were estimated using activity-based analysis for care, rehabilitation, diagnosis and treatment, instruction and hospitalisation. The primary effect measure was self-reported health-related quality of life of patients over the period. The investigators adopted a hospital perspective in the analysis.

After multivariable adjustment, the investigators reported a clinically relevant lower average cost of €328 (95% CI: 20; 636) per patient in the interprofessional training unit compared with the conventional ward ($p = 0.037$). No statistically significant differences in quality of life were found between patients in either the interprofessional training unit or the conventional ward [adjusted difference of 0.01 (95% CI: −0.05, 0.05; $p = 0.691$)]. Replicated estimates of the incremental cost-effectiveness ratio revealed that interprofessional training unit intervention was superior to the conventional ward.

CONCLUSIONS

There is a lack of robust evaluations of medical curricula. Cost effectiveness is rarely considered in programme evaluations. General statements about cost effectiveness of IPE are meaningless because of the wide variability in costs and outcomes associated with the diverse nature of IPE activities. Although decisions to change practice should be made based on evidence, we acknowledge that educational interventions with intended long-term consequences are difficult to measure. Diminishing education and health-service budgets may raise the importance of cost effectiveness in educational programme evaluation.

REFERENCES

1. Reeves S, Zwarenstein M, Goldman J, *et al.* Interprofessional education: effects on professional practice and health care outcomes. *Cochrane Database Syst Rev.* 2008 Jan 23; 1: CD002213.

2. Zwarenstein M, Goldman J, Reeves S. Interprofessional collaboration: effects of practice-based interventions on professional practice and healthcare outcomes. *Cochrane Database Syst Rev.* 2009; **3**: CD000072. Available at: www.mrw.interscience. wiley.com/cochrane/clsysrev/articles/CD000072/frame.html (accessed June 2010).

3. Hammick M, Freeth D, Copperman J, *et al. Being Interprofessional.* Cambridge: Polity Press; 2009.

4. Barr H. Interprofessional education: today, yesterday and tomorrow. The Learning and Teaching Support Network for Health Sciences & Practice from the United Kingdom Centre for the Advancement of Interprofessional Education. Occasional Paper No. 1. 2002.

5. Kennedy I. The inquiry into the management of care of children receiving complex heart surgery at the Bristol Royal Infirmary. A report. 2001.

6. Great Britain. Parliament. House of Commons. Health Committee. *The Victoria Climbie Inquiry report: sixth report of session 2002-03; report, and formal minutes together with oral evidence.* London: Stationery Office; 2003. 33p.

7. Donaldson L. *150 Years of the Chief Medical Officer's Annual Report 2008.* London: Department of Health; 2009.

8. Bennett C. *A Healthier Future for All Australians – final report of the National Health and Hospitals Reform Commission.* Canberra; 2009 June.

9. Hughes L. Creating an interprofessional workforce: an education and training framework for health and social care. 2007. Available at: www.caipe.org.uk/silo/ files/cipw-fw-doc.pdf (accessed June 2010).

10. Barr, op. cit.

11. CAIPE. Centre for Advancement of Interprofessional Education. Available at: www. caipe.org.uk (accessed June 2010).

12. CIHC. Canadian Interprofessional Health Collaborative. Available at: www.cihc.ca (accessed 6 November 2009).

13. EIPEN. European Interprofessional Education Network. Available at: www.eipen. org (accessed 6 November 2009).

14. Barr H, Koppel I, Reeves S, *et al. Effective Interprofessional Education: assumption, argument and evidence.* London: Blackwell; 2005.

15. Cooper H, Carlisle C, Gibbs T, *et al.* Developing an evidence base for interdisciplinary learning: a systematic review. *J Adv Nurs.* 2001; **35**(2): 228–37.

16. Hammick M, Freeth D, Koppel I, *et al.* A best evidence systematic review of interprofessional education. Best evidence medical evaluation review guide 9. *Med Teach.* 2007 Oct; **29**(8): 735–51.

17. Reeves S. A review of the effects of interprofessional education on staff involved in the care of adults with mental health problems. *J Psychiatr Ment Health Nurs.* 2001; 8(6): 533–42.

18. Reeves, Zwarenstein, Goldman, op. cit.

19. Ibid.

20. Bennett, op. cit.

21. Kirkpatrick DL. *Evaluating Training Programs: the four levels.* San Francisco, CA: Berrett-Koehler; 1994.

22. Barr H, Freeth D, Hammick M, *et al. Evaluations of Interprofessional Education: a United Kingdom review of health and social care.* London: CAIPE; 2000.

23. Barr, op. cit.

24. Ibid.
25. Ibid.
26. D'Amour D, Oandasan I. *Interprofessional Education for Patient-Centred Practice: an evolving framework.* Ottawa: Health Canada; 2004.
27. Hansen T, Jacobsen F, Larsen K. An evaluation of a training unit in Denmark. *J Interprof Care.* 2009; **23**(3): 234–41.
28. Ibid.

CHAPTER 6

Cost-effective e-learning in medical education

John Sandars

Someday, in the distant future, our grandchildren's grandchildren will develop a new equivalent of our classrooms. They will spend many hours in front of boxes with fires glowing within. May they have the wisdom to know the difference between light and knowledge.

—Plato

INTRODUCTION

The last decade has seen the rapid and relentless introduction of the Internet and information technology (IT) in undergraduate medical education, postgraduate medical education and continuing professional development. The costs of computers and connectivity to the Internet have dramatically fallen, but the use of multimedia to develop educational content and the supporting infrastructure to store and deliver this content usually requires substantial financial investment. Most of these costs are 'front end' and need to be paid before any content can be delivered to learners. However, there have been claims of incredible monetary savings in the commercial sector for the use of e-learning for training. Strother provides several examples such as IBM who apparently saved $200 million dollars in 1999 and was able to provide five times the learning at only one-third of the cost.[1]

It is not surprising that cash-strapped healthcare education providers are seduced by the thought of massive potential cost savings by the use of e-learning in medical education. An important question by medical education providers is whether e-learning is cost effective in this particular context. The concept of cost effectiveness initially appears to be simple—it considers the costs required to provide a desired outcome. However, the associated issues are more complex. This chapter will discuss the difficulties that are inherent in the measurement of cost effectiveness of e-learning in medical education and will highlight the problems of identifying the effectiveness of this form of training and how the associated costs can be calculated. Finally, the future of cost-effective e-learning in medical education is discussed, and several practical approaches to overcome the identified difficulties are proposed.

WHAT IS E-LEARNING?

There is no universally accepted definition of e-learning, but all definitions imply that technology is used to enhance teaching and learning. The traditional vision of e-learning is to provide multimedia educational content that can engage the learner. This content is assembled as training packages that can be offered to the learner using a wide variety of technology, from web sites, podcasts, CD-ROMs and a range of mobile devices, including personal digital assistants (PDAs) and mobile phones. Highly sophisticated simulations, virtual patients and immersive virtual worlds are also beginning to be developed for medical education.

Blended learning approaches are being increasingly used, in which the use of teaching and learning delivered by technology is mixed with face-to-face teaching. In these circumstances, e-learning often includes the use of quizzes and small discrete learning packages, known as reusable learning objects (RLOs), that can be used as additional resources to enhance existing teaching approaches.

Distance learning has been mainly replaced by online learning and technology (instead of the postal system) to deliver content. Entire training programmes can be provided through the Internet to remote learners and there is often some form of online discussion board. Occasionally, videoconferencing is used to link learners with tutors.

Recent technological advances have substantially reduced the entry level for anyone to create their own content, and this has led to the phenomenal growth of social software, such as blogs, wikis (e.g., Wikipedia), social-network sites (e.g., Facebook and Twitter) and media-sharing sites (e.g., YouTube and Flickr). In addition, there are powerful Internet search engines (e.g., Google and Yahoo!) that can almost instantaneously identify web-based content. Some of this social software has already been integrated into more formal educational settings, but mostly it is used for the extensive informal learning, which is an important feature of the learning landscape of most healthcare students and professionals.

WHAT IS EFFECTIVE E-LEARNING IN MEDICAL EDUCATION?

The possibility of measuring the effect of a particular intervention allows its effectiveness to be determined. A widely used approach to evaluate any training intervention considers its impact at several levels: reaction, learning, behaviour and results.[2] A review published in 2005 noted that the majority of evaluation studies of e-learning in continuing medical education were only at the level of reaction and were based on participant satisfaction data.[3] There were few studies that demonstrated change in performance, and no studies were identified in this review that demonstrated that web-based continuing medical education was effective in influencing patient or health outcomes.

A recent meta-analysis of Internet-based learning in the health professions showed that there were large positive effects compared with no intervention, with the greatest effect for knowledge and skill outcomes but less for learner behaviours and patient outcomes.[4] The authors noted that the effects compared with non-Internet interventions were heterogeneous and generally small, suggesting that there was similar effectiveness between Internet and non-Internet interventions. One of the difficulties in measuring the effectiveness of e-learning in medical education is that often the training intervention is complex and includes aspects of face-to-face contact with tutors and both Internet delivery of learning content and online peer group discussion or tutoring. There has been little work that compares the effectiveness between different approaches of e-learning interventions.

Using newer technologies and social software for informal e-learning in medical education has been little researched, and only studies that considered the perceptions of users were identified at the time of writing, with no studies that measured the impact on learner behaviours and patient outcomes.[5]

The previous findings immediately beg the question of why e-learning should be used in medical education, and it is important to consider its effectiveness from the viewpoints of the different stakeholders. The use of e-learning has large potential benefits to learners, especially allowing them to take control over their learning. Learners can usually personalise their e-learning by choosing the time, pace, sequence and content of their learning experience. Other important aspects are the opportunity to work remotely and to fit in with busy domestic and professional responsibilities. There are also potential benefits for providers since identical high-quality learning content and approaches can be delivered to numerous learners once it has been initially prepared.

In summary, the evaluation of the effectiveness of e-learning in medical education depends on which stakeholder group is being considered. The importance of the learner perspective of the effectiveness of e-learning in medical education should not be disregarded. There has been little research about the use of newer approaches to informal e-learning in medical education.

WHAT ARE THE COSTS OF E-LEARNING IN MEDICAL EDUCATION?

The costs associated with e-learning in medical education can be considered to be direct and indirect. Direct costs are all those expenses related specifically to the provision of the e-learning training intervention. The costs are likely to vary substantially between the different approaches, with extremely high costs associated with high-fidelity simulations and virtual worlds. Most of the costs will be related to developing the intervention, and once it is developed there are lower operating or recurring costs that are mainly related to web hosting and administration.

Developing an e-learning intervention typically follows a development process.[6] The initial phases of deciding what to do and developing a prototype are highly intensive and require both content and technology experts. Few medical educators are skilled in using educational software packages, and often they require support to transform their ideas into a multimedia and interactive learning package. A prototype is invariably tested to ensure that there are no usability problems for learners, such as those related to ease of navigation or accessibility. The final version is then delivered to the learner. Delivery usually requires uploading and storing the learning package on a web site from which the learner can download when required. Direct costs are mainly related to staff time (content developers and technical experts), but the initial technical set-up with computers and software may also be high.

Indirect costs are those expenses that are not specifically related to the provision of the e-learning intervention but are necessary for the organisation to function, such as utilities and rent. The depreciation costs of computers and Internet servers are often high, but connectivity to the web is usually low to providers.

There are direct costs to learners, such as wages for the time spent on training, but they may also have to provide their own computers and Internet connection. The associated indirect costs to the learner also include equipment depreciation, and an important hidden cost is that they often work from home and have to pay for heating, lighting and rent.

In sum, the cost of e-learning in medical education includes both provider and learner costs. Provider costs are mainly for the initial development and include both people and technology costs. The hidden costs to the learner are usually ignored.

WHAT IS COST-EFFECTIVE E-LEARNING IN MEDICAL EDUCATION?

Cost effectiveness implies that for a given monetary expenditure, effective learning, especially change in professional behaviour and improved patient care, can be quantified. This should allow comparisons to be made between different training interventions, especially between e-learning and face-to-face training. There is often the assumption that once an e-learning intervention has been developed, the recurring costs are low, whereas face-to-face courses usually have a relatively low initial cost but this cost continues over the repeated future delivery of the intervention.

No reviews of the cost effectiveness of e-learning in medical education were identified, but two studies of the cost effectiveness of videoconferencing offer an insight into this important aspect of medical education.[7,8] Both studies were performed in remote locations with small numbers of participants. Evaluation of the impact in both studies was limited to change in knowledge scores and perceived change in competence and impact on practice. Participants highly rated the sessions in both studies. One study only measured the telecommunications costs. The other study of physical and occupational therapists attempted to identify cost effectiveness. This study showed that there was no difference in the learning impact between a face-to-face full-day training workshop and videoconferencing, but there was a 'considerable' cost savings to both participants and the healthcare organisation that provided the training. A cost savings of at least 7 347 Canadian dollars was suggested.

There are numerous studies of cost effectiveness of e-learning in a diverse range of commercial organisations and invariably they show a high cost-benefit.[9] Most of these evaluations are case studies that have been produced by commercial third-party vendors of e-learning training. The main purpose is for marketing since the business world usually buys e-learning interventions from vendors, and they have to justify the high initial expenditure compared with their own in-house face-to-face training. Usually, there is similar effectiveness between e-learning and face-to-face training. The increased cost effectiveness of e-learning is based on the reduced costs of the learner's time away from work, and the subsequent loss of productivity, as well as the travel costs, which can be substantial for multinational businesses. It is interesting to note that there is often a transfer of costs to the learner when e-learning is used, since time for online study may be uncompensated non-work time and the equipment to access the e-learning training may be personal. These hidden costs are usually ignored in the calculation of cost effectiveness.

An important consideration for e-learning is that of opportunity cost. Opportunity cost is the cost of the alternative that is the 'next best' option when choosing a certain action or decision. The use of e-learning is rarely the only alternative choice to providing training, and usually, a deliberate decision is made to use e-learning instead of another approach, such as a lecture or workshop.

In summary, there is little research that considers the cost effectiveness of e-learning in medical education, but there have been a large number of studies in commercial organisations.

WHAT IS THE FUTURE FOR COST-EFFECTIVE E-LEARNING IN MEDICAL EDUCATION?

It is surprising that there has not been more interest in evaluating the cost effectiveness of e-learning in medical education, especially with its rapid and widespread uptake as an educational approach at both undergraduate and postgraduate levels, including continuing professional development. In the present economic climate, it seems highly likely that this position will not continue and cost effectiveness will need to be urgently addressed. The challenge to make e-learning cost-effective in medical education can be simplistically responded to by either reducing the cost or increasing its effectiveness. Both of these options are possible, and some aspects are already being implemented but more needs to happen.

The main cost of e-learning is the initial development of learning content, especially if it contains multimedia presentations or animation. Sharing content between providers is an obvious answer to reduce these costs, and there are several initiatives but these schemes are not without problems. Most providers will not willingly share content on which they have spent time and money developing unless there is some form of reciprocal agreement. An example is International Virtual Medical School (IVIMEDS), which is a worldwide collaboration of medical schools that provides access and sharing of high-quality learning content that individual medical schools can assemble into their own customised courses. However, there are a few providers who offer free content, such as Johns Hopkins' OpenCourseWare (OCW). One major difficulty of sharing content is that it may be unusable in different contexts, either because it does not easily align with the intended use (e.g., an animation of the heart may only show one aspect of the cardiac cycle when another aspect is required), or there may be technical problems with interoperability that do not allow learning objects to be used across different delivery systems or web sites. There are still unresolved major issues related to copyright and intellectual property rights, although ventures such as Creative Commons are beginning to clarify this complex position, especially when there is international sharing of content. Creative Commons offers a voluntary approach for authors of content to clearly state whether they wish to restrict or waive copyright for certain materials.

The cost of developing e-learning content can be reduced by replacing high-cost multimedia presentations with more simple approaches, such as audio podcasts that can be listened to on digital media players or most mobile phones. There has been little work to identify the preferences of learners or to compare the effectiveness between the different e-learning approaches.

Improving the effectiveness of e-learning in medical education should have a focus on improving the intervention to produce the desired impact, either on changing clinical behaviour or improving patient outcomes. Some e-learning providers have anecdotal tales about how they have either not made best use of the development money or they have provided a product that learners have not found useful or usable. These problems can be reduced by paying careful attention to quality standards for e-learning, such as clearly identifying the learning needs of the target audience, ensuring that the intended learning outcomes can lead to change in professional behaviour, aligning technology to best support these outcomes, scaffolding the learning experience so that there is active learning and engagement of the learner, providing institutional and tutor support, providing learner support and constantly evaluating the process so that iterative changes can occur.[10] Evaluation is an essential component of achieving high-quality e-learning, but often it is insufficiently funded at the time of obtaining the funding for the development of the content. The learner experience is fundamental to any evaluation of e-learning since this appears to be the main advantage over face-to-face learning. Key aspects of this evaluation are its perceived usefulness, including learning content and the opportunity to individualise the learning experience, and especially its usability (i.e., the ease of use of the technological delivery).

The use of new technologies and social software appear to have minimal cost, but there are major concerns about the quality of the learning experience for medical education. Most educators would agree that Facebook and YouTube are not ideal learning resources for content, but there are other aspects that must be considered. An important aspect of professional learning is responding to the problems that arise in the complex world of practice. Professionals want to obtain information, share opinions and receive support from their peer group and other professionals. Opportunities for this 'community of learners' to meet face-to-face are becoming increasingly difficult, but online networks and communities can flourish through the new opportunities offered by social software.[11]

It is likely that the relationship between tutor and learner will change with the more widespread use of e-learning in medical education. The tutor is less likely to be a 'sage on the stage' and more a 'guide on the side' that facilitates learning by directing the healthcare professional to the wide range of learning opportunities that are easily and freely available on the web. There is a massive and ever-increasing variety of resources that includes clinical and managerial web sites, podcasts, blogs written by both healthcare professionals and patients, videos on YouTube and professional chat rooms. Professional learning will occur by combining these multiple resources in response to individual learning needs that have been identified in the course of daily professional practice. A truly personalised learning experience can be created at minimal direct cost.

CONCLUSIONS

There has been little evaluation of the cost effectiveness of e-learning in medical education. The present economic climate is likely to see increasing demands made by a wide range of provider stakeholders, from governments and policy makers to commercial organisations and pharmaceutical companies, to justify the costs of e-learning. Proving that e-learning is more effective than alternative training interventions may prove to be elusive, especially if learner behaviours and patient outcomes are the main measures of effectiveness. The main benefit of e-learning for both providers and learners is that it can provide consistent quality of content at a time and a place that is convenient to both parties. Learners can undoubtedly begin to balance the complexities of social, personal, family and professional lives that are typical in the 21st century. Providers no longer have to deliver training at distant venues to small numbers of students, and they can easily individualise learning opportunities to specific learners or groups of learners. It will be essential to robustly evaluate the costs of e-learning in medical education so that the reports of enormous cost savings in the commercial world can be tempered to the healthcare context. Realistic evaluation of the true costs of e-learning in medical education can consider factors such as productivity, with increased time for patient care and studying from home. The time appears ripe for a major evaluation of the cost effectiveness of e-learning in medical education.

REFERENCES

1. Strother JB. An assessment of the effectiveness of e-learning in corporate training programs. *Int Rev Res Open Dist Learn.* 2002; **3**(1): 1–14.
2. Kirkpatrick DL. *Evaluating Training Programs: the four levels.* 2nd ed. San Francisco, CA: Berrett-Koehler; 1998.
3. Curran VR, Fleet L. A review of evaluation outcomes of web-based continuing medical education. *Med Educ.* 2005; **39**(6): 561–7.
4. Cook DA, Levinson AJ, Garside S, *et al.* Internet-based learning in the health professions: a meta-analysis. *JAMA.* 2008; **300**(10): 1181–96.
5. Sandars J, Schroter S. Web 2.0 technologies for undergraduate and postgraduate medical education: an online survey. *Postgrad Med J.* 2007; **83**(986): 759–62.
6. Ivers KS, Barron AE. *Multimedia Projects in Education: designing, producing, and assessing.* 3rd ed. Westport, CT: Libraries Unlimited; 2005.
7. Allen M, Sargeant J, Mann K, *et al.* Videoconferencing for practice-based small-group continuing medical education: feasibility, acceptability, effectiveness, and cost. *J Contin Educ Health Prof.* 2003; **23**(1): 38–47.
8. Miller PA, Huijbregts M, French E, *et al.* Videoconferencing a stroke assessment training workshop: effectiveness, acceptability, and cost. *J Contin Educ Health Prof.* 2008; **28**(4): 256–69.
9. Broadbent B. *ABCs of E-Learning.* San Francisco, CA: Josey-Bass/Pfeiffer; 2002.
10. Wong G, Greenhalgh T, Russell J, *et al.* Putting your course on the web: lessons from a case study and systematic literature review. *Med Educ.* 2003; **37**(11): 1020–3.
11. Sandars J, Haythornthwaite C. New horizons in medical education: ecological and Web 2.0 perspectives. *Med Teach.* 2007; **29**(4): 307–10.

CHAPTER 7

Cost-effective face-to-face learning

John Spencer and John Pearson

I will gladly lecture for fifty dollars, but I'll not be a guest for less than a hundred.
—Elbert Hubbard

INTRODUCTION

The concept of cost effectiveness—whereby something is deemed 'effective or pro-ductive according to cost'[1]—depends crucially on being able to define a discrete effect or outcome that can then be costed. This immediately presents a problem in the context of face-to-face learning in medicine, which, especially in the clinical environment, is complex. Outcomes can be short term or may be 'wide, long and deep'[2] and are usually attained across several domains, including cognitive, psycho-motor, emotional or behavioural.[3] Today's basic science undergraduate lecture may seem irrelevant; however, later in the course of a student's medical education, when this prior knowledge is activated and retrieved at the bedside of a real patient and their problem(s), it will make sense. This, along with an historical paucity of valid and reliable tools for assessing educational effectiveness, may be one of the reasons that cost-effectiveness analysis has generally been overlooked in evaluation of medi-cal education.[4] Similarly, costing education is problematic, either at the level of a single teaching session or a whole programme.

The range of settings in which face-to-face learning takes place in medicine is wide; the main ones are listed in Box 7.1 and can be classified into physical settings (in the classroom, in the workplace and in the community) and virtual settings.

Teaching and learning in these different settings may be one-to-one, one-to-several (between five and ten being considered the ideal size for a small group), peer-to-peer and multiprofessional. This chapter will explore aspects of cost effectiveness in rela-tion to each of the different settings.

Box 7.1 Settings in which face-to-face learning takes place in medicine

Classroom
    Lecture hall
    Seminar room
    Science laboratory
    Skills lab/simulation centre
Workplace
    Ambulatory clinic
        General practice/family medicine
        Hospital-based/outpatients
    Inpatient hospital ward
        Ward round
            Dedicated teaching round
            Business round
        Dedicated bedside teaching
    Other
        Operating theatre
        Emergency room
Community (e.g., patient's home)
Virtual

EVALUATING EDUCATIONAL EFFECTIVENESS

Evaluating the effectiveness of an educational intervention requires careful fore-thought and planning followed by rigorous execution, yet it is often treated lightly (e.g., distributing a hastily constructed questionnaire at the end of a teaching session). Evaluation has political, ethical and methodological dimensions, depending on its intended purpose and for whom it is being undertaken. Thus, if it is going to give meaningful answers, as with research, detailed consideration must be given to aims, methods, choice of outcome methods, analysis and dissemination.[5] However, historically, much evaluation in medical education has been undertaken in the short term and at fairly 'low' levels (e.g., assessing learner satisfaction or self-reported attainment of learning outcomes, gains in knowledge and skills and so on). Although this information may be useful (e.g., for internal quality-assurance purposes, as stated earlier), it does not really help inform discussions about cost effectiveness.

ASSUMPTIONS IN COSTING EDUCATION

There is no standard formula, but in relation to face-to-face learning, costs can be divided into the following categories.

Direct costs

- Teacher time (including preparation time) and on-costs (paid by the employer, such as superannuation).
- Teaching materials (handouts, equipment and mannequins).
- Technology (hardware and videolinks).
- Administrative, clerical and technical support.

Indirect costs

- Costs of any effect that teaching has on other processes (e.g., slowing down throughput of patients in a clinic).
- Organisational overheads, such as human-resource costs.
- Operational costs of maintaining 'plant' (teaching space and equipment).
- Costs borne by the learners, not only obvious costs such as travel expenses but also opportunity costs if there are competing demands on their time.
- In clinical education, costs borne by patients, also including opportunity costs.

THE CLASSROOM

The lecture

The lecture is one of the most ubiquitous and enduring teaching methods; indeed, historically, along with bedside teaching, it has been the mainstay of medical education at both undergraduate and postgraduate level. In the past couple of decades, however, the lecture has attracted a 'bad press', epitomised by the wag's definition: 'The transference of the notes of the lecturer to the notes of the student without passing through the brains of either' (anonymous). The rise in popularity of small groups, particularly in relation to problem-based learning (PBL), has been accompanied by a parallel decline in the lecture's reputation. Undoubtedly, the lecture is a waste of time and resources when delivered in an uninspiring way, the monotonous narrative supplemented by too many 'busy' slides (also known as 'death by PowerPoint'). The audience is passive, and the format perpetuates the model of teacher as gatekeeper of knowledge rather than facilitator of learning. On the other hand, 'a lecture can be effective and efficient, particularly if given by an expert in the domain because it enables them to embed new knowledge in a meaningful context'.[6] Good lecturers will actively engage learners using a variety of techniques, intuitively model professional attitudes and thinking, and will link theory and practice and bring concepts to life through stories. They will communicate enthusiasm for the subject, provide a scaffold on which learners can construct new knowledge, stimulate further inquiry and may actually be more up-to-date than other sources of information, such as textbooks or even the Internet. Indeed, they may provide information not available from any other sources. In terms of cost effectiveness, the lecture therefore has some appeal, particularly in a climate of budgetary constraints, increased student numbers and increasing pressures on academic staff. The physical resources are straightforward: an adequately sized classroom or lecture hall and relevant teaching materials and media (e.g., projector to connect with a computer). The main direct cost will be the lecturer's time.

There is little research evidence to support the choice of lectures over other approaches on economic grounds. However, Belfield and Brown published a review in which they attempted a cost-effectiveness analysis of lectures compared with a range of alternative approaches: personalised instruction, discussion modes, independent study and 'other modes'.[7] Their source of data about educational effectiveness (usually expressed as an effect size) was Bligh's seminal work on 'the lecture' (quoted in Belfield and Brown, 2002). Estimated costs included provider time, including time for preparation, 'hardware physical inputs' (e.g., premises and overheads), 'software physical inputs' (e.g., learning materials) and student effort. Generally, and unsurprisingly, provider costs constituted the bulk (around two-thirds) of the total costs across all studies. In terms of educational effectiveness, Bligh estimated that in over half of the studies, there was no significant difference, and that lectures were more effective than other modes in just over a quarter and less effective in one-fifth of studies. Taking all this into account, Belfield and Brown concluded that 'Based on experimental evidence, there is no mode of education that is more clearly cost-effective than lectures for imparting information'.[8] However, a teacher may aspire to more, or different, outcomes than simply 'imparting information' and will turn to other instructional approaches.

The small group

Although learning in a small group at the bedside has a long tradition, small groups in the classroom have only relatively recently gained prominence in medical education, particularly in the past two or three decades. A wide range of educational benefits are claimed, including attainment of 'higher order' cognitive outcomes such as evaluation and problem solving. Interpersonal and communication skills can be developed, attitudes challenged and collaborative working promoted. Through active participation in a supportive environment and with clear goals, learning is inevitably 'deep'.[9] In this respect, small-group learning 'trumps' large-group learning. However, effectiveness depends upon several important factors. Sessions need to be carefully planned to match tasks and methods with intended outcomes. Resource material needs to be developed, problems anticipated and strategies for dealing with them thought through. The skills of the facilitator are paramount; he or she must create a climate conducive to learning, attending not only to the task(s) but also to the needs of the group. This requires a flexible approach and a repertoire of communication skills, including attentive listening, questioning and constructive feedback. It also demands that certain conditions (organisational, physical, psychological and interpersonal) are established from the start. As with any approach, however, small-group teaching can be ineffective; common problems include the

session becoming a platform for a 'mini-lecture' by the tutor, lack of clarity about tasks and group dysfunction.

Since many more facilitators and facilities (not least, classrooms) are required for small-group than for large-group teaching, direct costs will inevitably be higher, increasing as student numbers rise. As with the lecture, there has been little, if any, economic evaluation of small-group learning.

The costs of a new PBL graduate entry course in Ireland were estimated[10] using the following assumptions: a student/tutor ratio of 8:1; tutors who were all medically qualified and 'reasonably well remunerated for their work' in providing 5 hours of tutoring per week; and multiple users of rooms (i.e., rooms to be used at different times by different users). The authors estimated start-up and recurring costs—unsurprisingly, tutor fees made up 89% of the latter. They acknowledged that using other clinicians (e.g., junior doctors or nurses) or nonclinical tutors and increasing student/tutor ratios would significantly reduce costs but could affect the quality of the learning experience.

THE WORKPLACE

Learning in the workplace (i.e., the clinical environment) has many advantages. It focuses on real-life problems in the context of professional practice, which motivates through its relevance. Its experiential nature is a powerful learning approach; professional thinking and attitudes can be modelled; and there are opportunities for individual, team and interprofessional learning.[11] It has everything going for it, yet many problems have been identified with clinical teaching, so much so that it has been described as a 'conceptually sound learning model, unfortunately flawed by problems of implementation'.[12] Commonly reported problems include its haphazard nature and consequent variability, lack of intellectual challenge, limited emphasis on problem-solving, poor feedback and 'teaching by humiliation'.[13] In mitigation, the challenges are considerable, not least that of trying to balance the needs of learners against the demands of caring for patients. There are significant time pressures; teaching is often opportunistic making planning difficult, and patients may be unwilling or unsuitable (e.g., too sick) to be involved.

Ambulatory settings

There has been increasing emphasis on education in ambulatory settings such as hospital outpatient clinics, emergency rooms, clinical investigation units and primary care and community clinics. The more apparent challenges in these setting are simultaneously caring for patients (often more than one at a time, and with needs that must be addressed before they leave the clinic) and teaching while under severe time constraints. Learning in an ambulatory setting has many potential benefits, however, including the opportunity for contact with a large number of patients, who are generally less sick than inpatients, and seeing problems in various stages of evolution.[14] Sadly, learning opportunities may be missed because of a combination of factors, well described in the literature: learners may end up as passive observers rather than actively involved; unpredictability and chaotic organisation (e.g., missing notes, unscheduled patients and so on); rapid throughput of patients; and inadequate physical space.[15] The key is good communication and planning, including anticipating problems and having contingencies ready for dealing with the unexpected. Good organisation involves orienting both students and staff (who are often junior and may not normally be involved in teaching), and carefully reviewing and planning patient flow and sequencing.[16] A variety of organisational models have been described, depending on the number of teachers, students and the location. They range from the 'grandstand' model, with multiple observers, to the 'report back' model, where learners see patients on their own and then report back. Occasional catch-up slots in a clinic may seem something of a luxury, indeed may extend the length of the clinic, but will help enhance the learning experience, prevent the clinic running too late and possibly help lower the clinician's stress levels. Simple strategies for efficient and effective time-limited teaching have been described: identify learners' needs; use a technique such as the '1-minute preceptor' for rapid, focussed teaching; encourage students to take responsibility for their learning; and give feedback, preferably based on observation.[17] Learners can take on a number of roles, ranging from simply observing (which, as mentioned earlier, is an-all-too-common 'default' situation and potentially very passive) to seeing their 'own' patients in parallel with the main clinic. The latter obviously is more demanding of the clinical teacher but provides a powerful experience.

Dedicated ambulatory care teaching centres have been advocated; these are essentially outpatient clinics with longer appointment times for preselected patients, so they can be involved in teaching at the same time as receiving care. No economic evaluation of such arrangements has been published.

At the bedside

Learning at the bedside, at its best, potentially ticks all the boxes for a powerful experience, providing 'an opportunity for the multidisciplinary team to listen to the (patient's) narrative and jointly interpret his concerns. From this unfolds diagnosis, management plans, prognosis formation and the opportunity to explore social, psychological, rehabilitation and placement issues'.[18] At worst, however, bedside teaching can be '...chaotic and frustrating... as students of varying levels of sophistication and interest fight off (or surrender to) interruptions and urges to go to sleep, while the attending physician holds forth on unanticipated topics and about patients who may not be available'.[19] There are a number of possible formats: the ward round, whether organised specifically for teaching purposes or a 'business' round, with or without pre- and post-round meetings; dedicated teaching sessions with selected patients; and students clerking patients, carrying out procedures, both supervised and unsupervised. The teaching may move between the bedside and classroom (or the ward corridor).

Despite the potential, there are several challenges. It is generally a very busy environment. The involvement of students may compromise the welfare and safety of sick patients, contemporary concerns focussing on infection control. Patient turnover may be high, making continuity difficult to achieve, and there is also potential for exploitation of patients and abuse of their goodwill if they are not given the opportunity to give fully informed consent. Furthermore, the traditional ward round format may be intimidating, even demeaning for patients as their problems are discussed in public.

Learners, particularly on the traditional ward round, are often of mixed ability and experience, and some (usually the most junior) may feel they are a burden, indeed may feel positively unwelcome. Inexperienced teachers worry about being shown up in front of the patient.

Teachers have to be ready to exploit unexpected 'teaching moments', and one of the challenges, particularly on the 'business' type of ward round, is keeping learners actively involved, as problems are assessed and decisions made, usually at a fast pace. Learning opportunities are increased when time for discussion is built in, e.g., '3-minute round-ups' after the round away from the bedside.

Many studies of the attributes of effective teachers have taken place at the bedside. They are well prepared and organised, understand how students learn, provided a collaborative learning environment, actively involve the students, brief both the students and their patients, give constructive feedback, teach general rules and model professional behaviour. Students recognise these good teachers, identify them as positive role models and ultimately learn more from them.[20]

The operating theatre

The operating theatre (OT) is one of the most complex and challenging settings in which clinical education takes place. Student involvement might include anything from working with the anaesthetic team to scrubbing up and assisting. The potential for learning is huge. As one author put it, the OT 'provides a sensory perceptual experience enabling students to construct a "clinical memory", by integrating tactile sensations of live pathology with visual images and verbal learning. It presents an opportunity to observe real clinical problems and their surgical management, to begin to appreciate what surgery means to patients both physically and emotionally and gain insights into the work of the surgeon as a member of a multiprofessional team'.[21] When it works, the experience is valuable, enjoyable and exciting. However, unlike most other situations in clinical education, the patient's needs are critical and immediate. There may also be considerable tension due to the demands of the surgery, and the student is not only a possible hindrance to the surgical team but also may be a hazard. Unfortunately, for many students, the environment is experienced as alien and hostile; they find themselves competing with other learners whose needs are more pressing (e.g., the surgical trainee), learning is passive, and the opportunity is missed. At worst, and somewhat caricatured, the hapless student stands on the edge of action, with little clue about what is happening and who the various people are, is not spoken to except when curtly told not to stand there or do that, and when finally allowed to peer into the operating area is berated by the surgeon for not knowing any anatomy. A model of learning in the OT proposes that if students are to benefit, they must successfully negotiate several challenges. These include making judgements about the relevance (and thus opportunity costs) of attending theatre; and working out the social dynamics, all this against a background of anxiety about doing something wrong or being humiliated.[22] Practical steps, such as an orientation session, have been described to make the OT more teaching-friendly.

COSTING CLINICAL EDUCATION

In the UK National Health Service (NHS), a funding stream known as service increment for teaching (SIFT), or additional cost of teaching (ACT) in Scotland, was introduced in the 1970s as a way of trying to cover the additional service costs incurred by hospitals that had a significant role in teaching medical students, predominantly the traditional university-linked teaching hospital. It was derived from the excess costs of such hospitals over other hospitals, the assumption being that these costs were indeed explained by the presence of students, an assumption that, although it has some intuitive strength, has never been properly tested.[23] Over the years, there were several revisions of the way the money was calculated, none wholly satisfactory, and in 1990, a new general practitioner (GP) contract introduced a small payment for teaching medical students. A major report in 1995 recommended more innovative use of SIFT, including payments to GPs, that undoubtedly enabled much innovation.[24] In addition, the report also recommended that the funding was divided into so-called 'facilities' money (80% of the total, to support infrastructure costs) and 'placements' money (20%, which would follow the student). Moving SIFT arrangements onto a contractual basis helped medical schools in their quality assurance endeavours (i.e., attempts to look at cost effectiveness and value for money), but the distribution of SIFT and ACT has remained controversial, not least because a significant proportion of the money, predominantly facilities money, has not been used to support teaching, was never properly accounted for, and has become embedded in services.[25] At the time of writing, a major review of state funding of clinical education and training across all professions is under way, which will doubtless have significant ramifications.

THE COMMUNITY

Teaching and learning in the community has increased inexorably over the past 20 years, and general practice clinical placements are now required components of undergraduate curricula, indeed some medical schools have adopted a distinctly community-based orientation.[26] A wide range of potential educational benefits have been described, including dealing with undifferentiated problems, seeing health, disease and illness in its social and environmental context, understanding the impact of the problem on the person and their family and inculcating a sense of social responsibility and service.[27] When curricula expanded into the community, there were anxieties about whether general practice could 'come up with the goods'. In fact, GP placements are greatly valued by students, and although such teaching is not without cost,[28] it is generally considered value for money.

Medical students also visit and learn from patients in their homes, usually as part of a schedule of early clinical contact or a GP attachment. They may also be involved in community placements or projects (e.g., during public health rotations). Generally, such schemes are very well received by all parties and make an important contribution to both learners' professional and personal development. However, costs (e.g., travel) will be incurred either by the student or the institution, and there may be opportunity costs for the patient. Formal teacher input is minimised although there will invariably be some kind of debriefing or feedback session requiring teacher input and facilitation.

VIRTUAL LEARNING

Advances in technology and globalisation of education have led to an increase in the use of online learning, and thus of virtual groups, both synchronous (i.e., interacting in real time) and asynchronous; the latter will not be considered here. The main differences between actual and virtual face-to-face groups include: obvious dependence on technology; the physical context, notably location; the timing and immediacy of interactions; and opportunities to record and archive discussions. There are also obvious communicative differences, notably the modification or suppression of nonverbal signals, and it has been argued that participants in virtual groups need 'to learn how to collaborate all over again', with communication lying 'somewhere between the formality of the written word and informality of the spoken'.[29] Online discussion, however, may be of particular value for less-assertive learners.

Despite the aspects of virtual learning just described, it can be argued that there are more similarities than differences, in terms of both factors that promote effective function and factors that detract from it. Most of the structured group techniques described in the literature[30] can be adapted for use online. Planning is as important as in other contexts, and e-moderators should give forethought to how members will interact, how much input will be required from themselves and who will lead and summarise discussions. As with actual face-to-face groups, the early stages are crucial, and time invested by the e-moderator in articulating objectives, clarifying tasks, establishing ground rules and using icebreakers that encourage social interaction and personalisation of participants will be time well spent. Participants also need time to become acquainted with the technology and need clear guidelines about modes of collaboration. Availability of technical support is also important and represents a hidden cost.

The use of virtual groups has become a necessity in the context of a distributed curriculum when learners are geographically dispersed and potentially also appealing in respect of minimising the 'carbon footprint' of an educational programme. However, it is not a panacea and may be more useful for straightforward information exchange than when there is a need for significant emotional engagement or when important social and contextual clues that influence face-to-face communication and group dynamics might be missed. Encouraging active participation is a continual challenge.

PEER-TO-PEER

Learners have always come together spontaneously to study without a teacher; indeed peer learning groups are commonplace in postgraduate and professional settings. Now, student-led group working is gaining prominence as a formal component of undergraduate medical curricula[31] not only in recognition of its inherent virtues but also because professional regulating bodies require graduates to gain experience in areas such as teamwork and teaching skills.[32] It may perhaps also be a response to increasing student numbers. Many benefits are claimed for so-called peer-assisted learning (PAL): it is self-evidently learner-centred; it fosters collegiality and collaboration; and it nurtures the development of skills such as facilitation. There are also potential educational gains—not least the value of learning through teaching but also positive effects on motivation. There are many variations on the theme; for example, group members may all be at the same stage or senior students may act as facilitators, instructors or mentors. There is theoretical support for PAL from cognitive, affective and organisational perspectives.[33] Disadvantages include learning being patchy or superficial and potential for dysfunction within groups. It is important to recognise that not all students are suited to the role of tutor, so they have to be carefully selected, then trained and supported. Another perhaps paradoxical potential disadvantage, and a hidden cost, is administrative and academic support that some PAL schemes seem to require.

FACULTY DEVELOPMENT

The historical assumption that if you were clinically competent and/or an expert in your field, you would automatically be able to teach effectively is disappearing. It is increasingly recognised that although some people are innately good teachers, most people need to learn how to teach. Faculty development is now seen as a central component of delivering a curriculum, and it is an expectation in medicine that teachers will be properly trained for the job.[34] However, despite a large literature, there is little evidence as to which faculty development approaches are most effective. Nevertheless, a Best Evidence Medical Education (BEME) review identified features of faculty development programmes that had been linked with positive outcomes: use of experiential learning; provision of feedback on performance; effective peer and colleague relationships; well-designed needs-based interventions; programmatic rather than one-off strategies; and use of a diversity of educational methods.[35] However, in the context of clinical education, given the number of teachers involved in a programme, the costs of a comprehensive faculty development programme could be considerable and represent a significant indirect cost. However, in light of evidence that good clinical teaching makes a difference—to learners' competence at least[36]—it is probably a sound investment.

CONCLUSIONS

For a variety of reasons, there have been few attempts at costing face-to-face learning in medicine. Cost-effectiveness analysis, particularly in respect of clinical education, is potentially bedevilled by the complexity of learning in the clinical environments, and by poor quality and short-term evaluation. However, it has been argued that only when the effectiveness of different educational programmes can be determined will we be in a position to consider cost effectiveness and hence meet one of the major agendas of funders of medical education.[37]

REFERENCES

1. www.askoxford.com/concise_oed/costeffective?view=uk (accessed March 2010).
2. Hamilton J. Outcomes in medical education must be wide, long and deep. *Med Teach.* 1999; **21**(2): 125–6.
3. Dornan T, Boshuizen H, King N, *et al.* Experience-based learning: a model linking the processes and outcomes of medical students' workplace learning. *Med Educ.* 2007; **41**: 84–91.
4. Belfield CR, Brown CA. How cost-effective are lectures? A review of the experimental evidence. In: Levin HM, McEwan PJ, editors. *Cost-Effectiveness and Educational Policy. AEFA Handbook.* Larchmont, NJ: Eye on Education; 2002.
5. Goldie J. Evaluating educational programmes. AMEE Education Guide No. 29. *Med Teach.* 2006; **28**: 210–24.
6. Custers and Boshuizen (quoted in Dornan and Ellway). Large group teaching. In: Dornan T, Mann K, Scherpbier A, *et al.*, editors. *Medical Education: theory and practice.* Elsevier; 2010 (in press).
7. Belfield, Brown, op. cit.
8. Ibid.

9. Dennick R, Spencer J. Teaching and learning in small groups. In: Dornan T, Mann K, Scherpbier A, *et al.*, editors. *Medical Education: theory and practice.* Elsevier; 2010 (in press).

10. Finucane P, Shannon W, McGrath D. The financial costs of delivering problem-based learning in a new, graduate-entry medical programme. *Med Educ.* 2009; **43**: 594–8.

11. Spencer J. Learning and teaching in the clinical environment. ABC of learning and teaching in medicine. *BMJ.* 2003; **332**: 591–3.

12. Irby D. *Effective Clinical Teaching & Learning: clinical teaching and the clinical teacher.* Available at: www.med.cmu.ac.th/secret/meded/ct2.htm (accessed March 2010).

13. Irby D. Teaching and learning in ambulatory settings: a thematic review of the literature. *Acad Med.* 1995; **70**(10): 898–931.

14. Sprake C, Cantillon P, Metcalf J, *et al.* Teaching in an ambulatory setting. *BMJ.* 2008; **337**: a1156.

15. Irby, op. cit.

16. Sprake, op. cit.

17. Irby DM, Wilkerson L. Teaching when time is limited. *BMJ.* 2008; **336**: 384–7.

18. O'Hare JA. Anatomy of the ward round. *Eur J Intern Med.* 2008; **19**(5): 309–13.

19. Ramani S, Leinster S. Teaching in the clinical environment. AMEE Guide No. 34. *Med Teach.* 2008; **30**: 347–64.

20. Irby D, Papadakis M. Does good clinical teaching really make a difference? *Am J Med.* 2001; **110**: 231–2.

21. Lyon P. A model of teaching and learning in the operating theatre. *Med Educ.* 2004; **38**: 1278–87.

22. Ibid.

23. Clack GB, Bevan G, Eddleston ALWF. Service increment for teaching (SIFT): a review of its origins, development and current role in supporting undergraduate medical education in England and Wales. *Med Educ.* 1999; **33**: 350–8.

24. Ibid.

25. Bevan G. The medical service increment for teaching (SIFT): a £400m anachronism for the English NHS? *BMJ.* 1999; **319**: 908–11.

26. Howe A, Campion P, Searle J, *et al.* New perspectives—approaches to medical education at four new UK medical schools. *BMJ.* 2004; **329**: 327–31.

27. Spencer J. What can undergraduate education offer general practice? In: Harrison J, van Zwanenberg T, editors. *GP Tomorrow.* 2nd ed. Oxford: Radcliffe Medical Press; 2002. Ch. 4.

28. Murray E, Jinks V, Modell M. Community-based medical education: feasibility and cost. *Med Educ.* 1995; **29**: 66–71.

29. Jaques D, Salmon G. *Learning in Groups. A handbook for face-to-face and online environments.* 4th ed. Oxford: Routledge; 2007.

30. Ibid.

31. Ross MT, Cumming AD. Peer-assisted learning. In: Dent JA, Harden RM, editors. *A Practical Guide for Medical Teachers.* 3rd ed. Edinburgh: Churchill Livingstone; 2007. Ch. 18.

32. General Medical Council. *Tomorrow's Doctors 2009.* London: GMC; 2009.

33. Ross, Cumming, op. cit.

34. General Medical Council, op. cit.

35. Steinert Y, Mann K, Centeno A, *et al.* A systematic review of faculty development initiatives designed to improve teaching effectiveness in medical education: BEME Guide No. 8. *Med Teach.* 2006; **28**: 497–526.
36. Irby, Papadakis, op. cit.
37. Murray E, Gruppen L, Catton P, *et al.* The accountability of clinical education: its definition and assessment. *Med Educ.* 2000; **34**: 871–9.

CHAPTER 8

Cost-effective simulation

Jean Ker, George Hogg and Nicola Maran

Experience teaches slowly and at the cost of mistakes.

—*James A Froude*

WHAT IS SIMULATION?

Simulation is the reproduction of all or some aspect of a job or task. This is generally recreated in an environment that is safe for the learner. McGaghie[1] describes simulation as 'a person, device or set of conditions that tries to present problems authentically. The student or trainee is required to respond to the problems as he or she would under natural circumstances'. When used appropriately, simulation can enhance learning in all domains—cognitive, psychomotor and affective—in preparing practitioners for clinical practice.[2]

Simulation is an inclusive term that incorporates a broad range of activities—from the use of part task trainers such as a venepuncture arm or a shoulder joint for injections to student immersion in re-creations of authentic healthcare settings and systems. It also encompasses the use of virtual reality.[3,4,5]

WHY USE SIMULATION?

Simulation can be used for a broad variety of purposes in healthcare to meet practitioner, patient and organisational expectations (*see* Box 8.1).

Simulation also enables practices to be observed and training needs to be identified in a realistic workplace environment without compromising patient care.[6,7] This reflects the increasing evidence of the influence of contextual factors on individual and team performances.[8,9]

Box 8.1 Purposes of simulation in healthcare

Rehearsal of practice
Redesign of roles or service
Regulation of skills
Research into most cost-effective practices
Renewal of infrequently used skills to maintain expertise
Risk reduction
Reinforcement of standards of clinical practice

Simulation can be used to rehearse management of common events or those events that clinicians rarely see in their professional clinical lifetimes but which require prompt and effective treatment and which can be lifesaving (e.g., malignant hyperpyrexia in the anaesthetised patient or the initial management of an obstructed airway in a road-traffic accident). Training can focus on both the technical aspects of practice and the nontechnical aspects of working, such as communication, teamwork, decision-making and situation awareness.[10]

The apprenticeship model of 'learning on the job' is no longer fit for purpose with the need to provide more intensive, focused training that simulation can provide—enabling practitioners to be better prepared for the realities of their practice. Simulation can also play a significant role in preparing clinicians for intimate examinations.[11]

PATIENT EXPECTATIONS

In healthcare, patients now expect that they will be cared for by a practitioner who has already received an appropriate level of training and experience. Practitioners also expect to be prepared to deliver high-quality, consistent care in environments where healthcare delivery is not the primary role, such as residential homes.

Patients are increasingly aware of the cost of mistakes both in terms of damage or loss of their lives or their livelihoods. Simulation provides the opportunity to re-create the significant event and explore through feedback and debriefing an analysis of the underlying causes as well as future preventative practices.[12]

ORGANISATIONAL NEEDS

Simulation has been used in many high-reliability organisations, most notably civil and military aviation, to try to decrease both systems and individual errors through rehearsal and structured progressive contextual learning opportunities.[13,14]

Although clearly expensive to deliver, simulation training is regarded as cost-effective because it enhances reliability of practice minimising the incidence of adverse events where it is simply too costly in human and financial terms to allow mistakes to be made.[15,16]

Simulation can also be used effectively at all levels of the organisation from the individual practitioner, whether novice or expert, to entire teams or even at the broadest institutional level. All aspects of healthcare—environmental, organisational and individual—can be safely explored, including the impact of change on the delivery of services.[17]

The opportunity for organisations to use simulation to ensure consistency of standards and plan for workforce development is cost-effective, as it enables them to rehearse and assess consequences both predicted and unforeseen before their full implementation.

WHAT DO WE KNOW ABOUT EFFECTIVE SIMULATION?

The evidence base for the effectiveness of simulation training in healthcare is both limited and sporadic. In a systematic review of high-fidelity simulation, Issenberg *et al.*[18] reported a number of key features that consistently facilitated learning. These included:

- providing feedback
- allowing repetitive practice
- integrating the use of simulation events within a curricular programme
- providing a range of difficulties and scenarios
- defining learning outcomes.

These features of effective simulation are echoed by Salas *et al.*[19]

Simulation provides an opportunity for deliberate practice[20] that enhances learning. The powerful learning than can be created through the use of simulation is also related to the debriefing process that occurs after the simulation event.[21] This enables practitioners to review their performance and critique it as part of their reflective practice.[22,23] This reflection can be augmented using video-assisted debriefing.

Emerging evidence of what enhances effectiveness in a simulation event has been reported.[24] The impact of using simulation on improving practitioners' performance in the workplace has identified that changes in practice (e.g., crisis management in anaesthesiology) were not limited to the specific clinical events used in the simulation training but transferred to other clinical scenarios.[25] Many studies of surgical simulation demonstrate that simulator training improves technical performance and reduces the number of errors. This is achieved through deliberate practice of specific procedures using simulation (virtual reality) that can detect, record and analyse near misses and errors without risk to patients.[26]

In other high-reliability industries, such as the military and aviation, there is a long history of incorporating simulation into education and training programmes,[27] for both technical skills as well as cognitive and social skills training for effective teamwork. The evidence that such training is effective in reducing accidents and incidents is, in fact, limited even in these fields. However, no other industry has felt it necessary to wait for such evidence to implement simulation training.

WHAT ARE THE OBVIOUS COSTS?

Simulation is very expensive, both financially and in terms of personnel time. The obvious costs of simulation can be categorised under the following:
- hardware
- learners
- faculty development
- facilities
- patients.

These categories can be analysed from political, economic, social and technological perspectives.

Hardware

The most obvious cost associated with simulation is that of purchasing the simulator hardware itself, some of which may be highly specialised. The market for medical simulation devices is growing rapidly and because of such demand the quality of products available is growing while the cost of available simulators is falling. This makes sophisticated simulators both affordable and accessible, which can create social costs in relation to skills centres being pressured to purchase manikins without identifying why they are required to enhance learning.

In addition to the economic costs of the specialist part task, mid- and high-fidelity simulators, there is also the cost of audiovisual equipment for debriefing and for enabling of reflection on practice[28]—one of the vital components of the effective use of simulation. This requires an electronic storage and transfer system because practitioners are increasingly required, as part of their continuing professional development or for the purposes of revalidation, to provide evidence of their learning. The rapid developments in technology, particularly in relation to wireless simulators (remotely operated and not physically attached to controls) and mobile technology [using a personal digital assistant (PDA) to record evidence of practice of procedures or using podcasts of clinical examinations on mobile telephones], also provide ongoing costs for simulation centres because the technology needs to be regularly reviewed and updated.

Learners

In terms of using simulation to train practitioners, there are the political costs of providing evidence to the professional regulatory bodies of standards related to the educational environment. This includes costs to simulation centres of having standard operating procedures and providing valid and reliable assessment tools. For learners, there is the cost of leave from the service to undertake simulation training to ensure that they are fit for purpose, given the new roles and changed responsibilities that are now core to service delivery. This is particularly costly, given the constraints of the European Working Time Directive and the costs to the healthcare organisation driven by government targets.

There are also social costs in relation to using simulation to enhance interprofessional learning and working. These often relate to the networking time required to establish interprofessional learning opportunities between different professional tutors. Simulation provides an opportunity to respond to political drivers to enhance teamwork.[29]

Faculty development

A further obvious cost is the cost of training the trainers to use simulators and to incorporate them into learning and teaching events to maximise learning and its transfer to practice.[30] Faculty are crucial to the effectiveness of simulation, particularly in relation to being professional role models as well as their specialist expertise in conducting simulations.

Facilities

Facilities for simulation training are also an obvious cost, particularly in relation to having the capability of re-creating an authentic healthcare environment with the increase in understanding of the impact of contextual factors on learning. For highly complex clinical scenarios, re-creating an authentic workplace environment with the appropriate engagement cues can be costly. There are a number of models for developing facilities, both fixed and mobile.[31]

Patients

Public expectations have changed over the past 40 years. Many patients have also become increasingly involved in the education of healthcare practitioners using simulation—either in real or simulated patient roles. The public have an increasing awareness of the training and education of competent healthcare practitioners, and many healthcare education organisations have lay members on their boards. For patients, the obvious (and welcome) cost of simulation is having the best-trained workforce delivering care.

WHAT ARE THE HIDDEN COSTS?

Hidden or indirect costs of using simulation can be considered under the following headings:
- hardware
- consumables

- learners
- faculty requirements
- facilities
- healthcare service.

Hardware

Although relatively reliable, simulators require upkeep in terms of component parts and maintenance, which often require a specialist-trained technician. This prevents the cost of damage and accidents to the simulators. Although some desktop simulation models will provide the learner with feedback, no matter how sophisticated the patient simulator, there is none capable of delivering training all by itself. And so, there are the technical costs of supporting the functioning of specialist audiovisual equipment and the cost of keeping trainers as well as the technical staff up to date, which are ongoing costs often overlooked in the enthusiasm to purchase the hardware.

All simulators have a 'natural lifespan'. This will vary depending on utilisation and in-house upkeep, but depreciation and replacement costs are often not considered. Although some manufacturers offer warranties, others charge for repairs as required.

Consumables

In order to create fidelity and reproduce the clinical tasks, consumables such as venflons, dressings, bedding and printed forms will be required and their replacement costs are often overlooked. Information technology (IT) programmes to support videodebriefing and storage of evidence will also require replacement and maintenance.

Learners

For those being trained using simulation, there are the hidden costs of backfill required to meet service requirements during training. Simulation requires quality management and control processes to be in place in order to ensure it supports both current and future service requirements. Ensuring that different healthcare practitioners are trained using simulation to a safe standard has costs in relation to addressing both current professional silo protectionist practices as well as the logistics of providing interprofessional learning opportunities. This includes identifying joint curricular time and tutors. There are the real costs of negotiation and collaboration in ensuring access to training for different health professional groups.

Another cost often not considered is the travel to a facility offering education and training using specialist simulation facilities.

Faculty requirements

In terms of the simulation event, the educational design and evaluation of the training can be considered a hidden cost because the whole event has to be created and detailed to maximise learning. The need to involve clinical experts in creating simulation scenarios is often not considered.

Facilities

One of the hidden costs of having purpose-built facilities for simulation training is the need for upgrades and refurbishment to ensure that teaching space is used to its maximum capacity. This often involves the costs of resource and administrative staff to ensure effective and efficient use of the facility. A simulated patient bank (often used to support simulation training) involves training, administration and travel expenses.[32]

WHAT IS COST-EFFECTIVE SIMULATION?

The cost of simulation-based training is high because of the expense of the simulator hardware or software and also because numbers of participants in each training episode are relatively low and instructor-to-learner ratios are high. However, in a climate where the public expect that healthcare practitioners will be trained before they undertake treatments or procedures on patients, there is no real alternative. Service changes in recent years do not provide a supportive environment for the apprenticeship model of learning for clinical practice.[33] Simulation can therefore be cost-effective in light of the reduction in the time available for training in clinical specialties.

The incidence of adverse events in healthcare is high, and the human cost of this is enormous in patients who die or are injured during treatment. The costs to the health service in terms of prolonged length of stay and readmissions following adverse events are high. In 2008–09, £1.5 billion was spent on patients being readmitted to hospital within a month[34] and recent figures suggest that £1 in £12 of the National Health Service (NHS) budget is spent on litigation.[35] The cost to the health service of inadequate training is clearly unsustainable. Although the evidence for effectiveness of simulation training in reducing such costs is not currently available, there is no other high-reliability profession that has waited for such evidence before adopting simulation into training programmes, because the cost of failure is simply too high.

Most evidence for the cost effectiveness of simulation in training and accreditation comes from the aviation domain where the number of hours of training required to achieve and maintain a licence to fly is strictly regulated. It is clear that the use of real aircraft for such purposes is much more expensive.[36] Orlanski and String[37] have demonstrated that the cost of training military personnel on a flight simulator is between 5% and 20% of the cost of using real aircraft for the purposes of training.

A study in Sweden demonstrated that junior surgeons who had been given virtual reality training for keyhole surgery made significantly fewer errors than their peers who had not. The untrained cohort took 58% longer to carry out a similar operation and on average made three times as many errors.[38] Apart from the obvious safety concerns, with current pressures to increase efficiency of operating theatre usage, there are clearly cost implications of allowing surgeons to learn such skills in the operating theatre.

Cost-effective simulation in clinical education involves providing the right educational experience at the right level at the right time to ensure the delivery of a quality experience. Simulation is only a tool that can be used effectively for educational delivery. In order to be effective, the tool must be used appropriately. This means ensuring that trainers are appropriately trained and educational products developed and tested to ensure best practice. The development of standards, such as those being developed by the Society for Simulation in Healthcare in the United States of America and by the Association for Simulated Practice in Healthcare in the United Kingdom, will help to quality assure simulation training for healthcare and ensure that the highest quality of education is delivered at the best price.

HOW DO WE MAKE SIMULATION MORE COST-EFFECTIVE?

The cost of simulators certainly increases as fidelity increases, and many make the mistake of thinking that the higher fidelity a simulation, the more will be gained from training. However, examples from other industries suggest that less can be more. There is evidence that some aspects of flying commercial jets are best taught using computer-based simulations rather than full-immersion simulators. Therefore, it is important to ensure that the correct simulator is being used for the training required. Indeed, some learning objectives may be met very effectively without using simulators at all.

Simulation is costly in terms of resources required, but a coordinated strategic approach by a healthcare organisation in relation to its use can prevent duplication of effort in relation to education and training. Many expensive simulators are purchased but not utilised to their maximum capacity. Sharing such simulators between educational institutions or across professional groups will help to maximise efficiency and indeed may lead to opportunities for multiprofessional learning.

Where simulation-based training is certified (such as cannulation or venepuncture training), quality assurance of the training delivered can allow transfer of such training from one institution or region to another, thus avoiding duplication.[39]

Regional or national networks also provide the opportunity to share resources, including both simulators and training resources. In a recent project funded by NHS Education for Scotland as part of a national skills and simulation strategy, access to skills using appropriate simulation techniques was ensured by developing a customised mobile unit with quality-controlled resources and training-the-trainer programmes. This ensured that practitioners had the opportunity to identify their own individual needs wherever they were practising.

CONCLUSIONS

Simulation is a costly but effective way of ensuring that reliable standards of practice are in place across the healthcare sector. It enables practitioners to update and enhance their technical and nontechnical skills, either individually or as a team across both common and rare clinical events without endangering patient care. With the advent of revalidation and changes in roles and responsibilities within the healthcare sector, the use of simulation is likely to increase. There are well-recognised costs related to staff and learner time as well as specialist equipment, but what is often not taken into account are the hidden costs to the healthcare service related to backfill and consumables. There are several examples where simulation is being used efficiently and effectively, but this is not universal across the health sector—which is required if its impact is to be maximal.

More research is required to build on the current knowledge base in relation to the cost effectiveness of simulation. This will require both infrastructure investment as well as a coordinated, collaborative approach to evaluate different models of simulation in practice.

REFERENCES

1. McGaghie WC. Simulation in professional competence assessment: basic considerations. In: Tekian A, McGuire CH, McGaghie WC, editors. *Innovative Simulations for Assessing Professional Competence*. Chicago, IL: Department of Medical Education, University of Illinois at Chicago; 1999. pp. 7–22.
2. Bradley P. History of simulation in medical education and possible future directions. *Med Educ.* 2006; **40**: 254–62.
3. Glavin RJ, Maran NJ. Integrating human factors into the medical curriculum. *Med Educ.* 2003; **37**(s1): 59–64.
4. Ker JS, Hesketh EA, Anderson F, *et al.* Can a ward simulation exercise achieve the realism that reflects the complexity of everyday practice junior doctors encounter? *Med Teach.* 2006; **28**(4): 330–4.
5. Ker J, Bradley P. *Simulation in Medical Education: ASME understanding medical education series.* Edinburgh: ASME; 2007.
6. Ker J, Mole L, Bradley P. Early introduction to interprofessional learning: a simulated ward environment. *Med Educ.* 2003; **37**(3): 248–55.
7. Hogg G, Pirie E, Ker JS. The use of simulated learning to promote safe blood transfusion practice. *Nurse Educ Pract.* 2006; **6**(4): 214–23.
8. Ostergaard HT, Ostergaard D, Lippert A. Implementation of team training in medical education in Denmark. *Qual Saf Health Care.* 2004; **13**(S1): i91–5.
9. Shapiro MJ, Morey JC, Small SD, *et al.* Simulation based teamwork training for emergency department staff: does it improve clinical team performance when added to an existing didactic teamwork curriculum? *Qual Saf Health Care.* 2004; **13**(6): 417–21.
10. Flin R, Maran N. Identifying and training non-technical skills for teams in acute medicine. *Qual Saf Health Care.* 2004; **13**(1): i80–4.

11. Pickard S, Baraitser P, Rymer J, *et al*. Can gynaecology teaching associates provide high quality effective training for medical students in the United Kingdom? Comparative study. *BMJ*. 2003; **327**(7428): 1389–92.
12. Kneebone RL, Scott W, Darzi A, *et al*. Simulation and clinical practice: strengthening the relationship. *Med Educ*. 2004; **38**(10): 1095–102.
13. Gaba DM. The future vision of simulation in health care. *Qual Saf Health Care*. 2004; **13**(1): i2–10.
14. Sexton J, Thomas E, Helmreich R. Error, stress, and teamwork in medicine and aviation: cross sectional surveys. *BMJ*. 2000; 320: 745–9.
15. Kohn LT, Corrigan JM, Donaldson MS. *To Err Is Human: building a safer health system*. Washington, DC: National Academy Press; 2000.
16. Department of Health. *An Organisation with a Memory*. London: Stationery Office; 2000.
17. Hogg G, Lorente M, Keith G, *et al*. The effectiveness of a ward simulation exercise to support hospital at night practitioners develop safe practice. *Int J Clin Skills*. 2008; **2**(2).
18. Issenberg SB, McGaghie WC, Petrusa ER, *et al*. Features and uses of high-fidelity medical simulations that lead to effective learning: a BEME systematic review. *Med Teach*. 2005; **27**(1): 10–28.
19. Salas E, Wilson KA, Burke CS, *et al*. Using simulation-based training to improve patient safety: what does it take? *Jt Comm J Qual Patient Saf*. 2005; **31**(7): 363–71.
20. Ericsson KA, Krampe RT, Tesch-Roemer C. The role of deliberate practice in the acquisition of expert performance. *Psychol Rev*. 1993; **100**(3): 363–406.
21. Savoldelli GL, Naik VN, Park J, *et al*. Value of debriefing during simulated crisis management: oral versus video-assisted oral feedback. *Anesthesiology*. 2006; **105**(2): 279–85.
22. Rogers J. *Adults Learning*. 4th ed. Maidenhead: Open University Press; 2001.
23. Schön D. *Educating the Reflective Practitioner*. San Francisco, CA: Jossey-Bass Publishers; 1987.
24. Dieckmann P, Rall M, Sadler C. What competence do simulation instructors need? *Minerva Anaesthesiol*. 2008; **74**: 277–81.
25. Weller J, Wilson L, Robinson B. Survey of change in practice following simulation-based training in crisis management. *Anaesthesia*. 2003; **58**(5): 471–3.
26. Seymour NE, Gallagher AG, Roman SA. Virtual reality training improves operating room performance: results of a randomised double-blind study. *Ann Surg*. 2002; **236**(4): 458–63.
27. Burke CS, Salas E, Wilson-Donnelly K, *et al*. How to turn a team of experts into an expert medical team: guidance from the aviation and military communities. *Qual Saf Health Care*. 2004; **13**(S1): i96–104.
28. Schön, op. cit.
29. Kyrkjebø JM, Brattebø G, Smith-Strøm H. Improving patient safety by using interprofessional simulation training in health professional education. *J Interprof Care*. 2006; **20**(5): 507–16.
30. Dieckmann, Rall, Sadler, op. cit.
31. NHS Education for Scotland, Scottish Funding Council Partnerships for Care, the Scottish Clinical Skills Strategy East Deanery, Dundee: 2007.
32. Ker JS, Dowie A, Dowell J, *et al*. Twelve tips for developing and maintaining a simulated patient bank. *Med Teach*. 2005; **27**(1): 4–9.

33. O'Neill PA, Willis S, Jones A. A model of how students link PBL with clinical experience through elaboration. *Acad Med.* 2002; 77(6): 552–61.
34. *The Dr Foster Hospital Guide 2009: how safe is your hospital?* Available at: www.drfoster health.co.uk/docs/hospital-guide-2009.pdf (accessed January 2010).
35. Department of Health Annual Report, England: HMSO; 2009.
36. Orlanski J, String J. *Cost Effectiveness of Computer Based Instruction in Military Training.* Alexandria, VA: Institute for Defense Analysis; 1977.
37. Ibid.
38. Chief Medical Officer. Annual Report Department of Health, England: HMSO; 2008.
39. Burke, Salas, Wilson-Donnelly, op. cit.

CHAPTER 9

Problem-based learning: is a cost-effective approach possible?

Gary Wittert and Adam Nelson

All models are wrong but some are useful.

—George Box

INTRODUCTION

The explosion of knowledge relating to the scientific basis and practice of medicine has necessitated changes in medical education. For example, an understanding of social equity and chronic-disease management and associated skills such as care planning, patient-centred care, motivational interviewing and behaviour change are required.[1] Graduating students must be capable of cooperative team-based behaviour, self-directed learning and knowledge transfer. There is also recognition that learning is best facilitated by a flexible range of approaches that meet individual student needs, in context, with a focus on important principles and with regular feedback. The required core knowledge, skills and outcome objectives are best defined by relevant professionals, and these need to be clearly communicated to students.[2]

Whether or not there is an optimal pedagogy is far more contentious. The costs of implementation and maintenance of a particular curriculum need to be considered and balanced against affordability; greater expenditure cannot be assumed to translate into better outcomes. Traditional lectures, small-group tutorials, laboratory and resource sessions as well as problem- and case-based learning all have useful roles in modern medical curricula. In addition, it is now increasingly apparent that e-learning can be used in a variety of ways to optimise knowledge acquisition, reasoning and problem-solving; it meets the needs of a generation of students acutely in tune with the capability and power of the medium. The balance between various forms of face-to-face and e-learning, and the extent to which students are afforded choice of learning methodology, remains to be determined. Interactive simulation devices are of increasing sophistication. The nature and mix of educational approaches will undoubtedly continue to evolve and ought to do so, informed by rigorous and ongoing research.

PROBLEM-BASED LEARNING: GENERAL PRINCIPLES

The overall goal of problem-based learning (PBL) as an educational methodology is to develop in students the principles of self-directed, life-long learning with a focus on clinical reasoning.[3,4] There is, however, considerable heterogeneity in what is meant by PBL. It originated, in its purest form, at McMaster University in 1968[5] and was not an adjunct or addendum to a curriculum but was the methodology used for the entire curriculum: its implementation was all or none.[6] The objectives of PBL were two-fold: first, to optimise the acquisition of a large body of knowledge in a manner that makes it most readily retrievable, and second, to develop self-directed learning capacity that allows students to extend this knowledge base when tackling unfamiliar problems in future clinical practice.[7] The educational concept was to provide a 'whole patient approach' to learning such that a clinical scenario would provide the vehicle for acquiring and integrating knowledge from all of the disciplines and skills required of a medical practitioner (e.g., physiology, anatomy, pathology, biochemistry, clinical chemistry, population health and communication skills); it represented a significant paradigm shift from the silo-based, subject and block learning of hitherto traditional curricula. In brief, the approach included the progressive presentation and elicitation of a clinical scenario, or patient, from historical details. The synthesis of the clinical problem, management and process of rehabilitation was elucidated over several successive, small-group sessions with self-directed learning by cooperative group effort, facilitated by a trained, preferably expert tutor. The underlying theory has been both adapted and selectively applied, and various 'forms' of PBL have evolved and been incorporated to varying extents in medical curricula around the world. For example, PBL has been implemented in medical schools with undergraduate entry programmes, whereas the original descriptions were based on work undertaken with scientifically trained postgraduates. In addition, it has been adapted for large groups (20–40 people) although it was originally designed for small groups (5–8 people), applied to clinical teaching when originally conceived for preclinical training, and has been facilitated by non-expert tutors when originally tutors were medically and specially trained. The varied forms of PBL and evolution of hybrid curricula have made assessment of the efficacy of PBL as a learning modality difficult and, at best, limited to individual universities. A broad appraisal of cost efficacy of a 'PBL curriculum' has similar limitations.

PBL: UTILITY AND COSTS

The widespread adoption of PBL in its varying forms and iterations has occurred in the absence of compelling evidence for its superiority over traditional curricula.[8] Moreover, there has been longstanding concern about the financial costs imposed by a PBL curriculum, but until relatively recently there has been little published data that quantifies those costs. Although there is considerable variation in what is meant by PBL and the approach used from institution to institution differs, the largest cost is always staff time. Accordingly, group size, number of groups and number of hours of PBL tutoring required per week are the most important determinants of cost.

The optimal group size is considered to be 6–8 people, and commonly in a typical week, there is about 6 hours of PBL divided into three sessions of 2 hours each. At one university, based on a group size of 8 people and 5 hours of PBL per week, and with the use of medically qualified tutors, the initial cost of delivering PBL was calculated as €1 526 952 (£1 369 138 or US$2 050 375), with an annual recurring cost of around €664 000/year, equating to €2767/student/year, 89% of which related to tutor salaries.[9] A fully integrated PBL curriculum is clearly an expensive exercise. PBL formats may be similarly effective for small (5–10) and large (10–40) groups, at least for postgraduate medical programmes. The evidence for this is based on a study that involved the provision of continuing medical education to primary care physicians using a PBL format in small (5–10 participants) and large (10–40 participants) groups of learners. The large- and small-group sessions were similarly enjoyed by most participants. There was a positive relationship between change in prescribing behaviour and length of the session but not the size of group. By self-report, 30%, 65% and 85% of participants were motivated to change prescribing behaviour after sessions of 1, 2 or 3 hours, respectively. The self-report data was corroborated by direct measurement of prescription writing, which showed that the physicians who participated in the PBL conferences recognised and treated asthma patients with a 50% greater use of inhaled corticosteroids than previously. The control group, which received didactic lecture-based teaching, did not show any increased prescription of corticosteroid medication.[10] At the undergraduate level, the University of Sheffield trialled a head-to-head comparison of traditional tutor-led small groups against a large-group 'integrated learning environment' to explore means of reducing staffing requirements.[11] In brief, 246 students were divided into 27 similar-sized small groups (9–11 people), five of which were randomised to undergo traditional-style PBL in small tutorial rooms with the remaining 22 groups randomised to the integrated learning environment. Each group randomised to the integrated learning environment, while physically altogether in one lecture theatre, worked independently through the PBL case over several sessions with two facilitators engaging the entire integrated learning environment in a discussion at the end of each session to demonstrate student understanding and to identify additional learning needs. Although only a short trial, the groups showed no significant difference in post-test knowledge and learning activity scores, suggesting that this large-group approach is equally as effective and, furthermore, that significant parts of the PBL process may successfully occur independent of intensive supervision or staffing. If some sessions or aspects of a PBL case can be delivered in similarly large groups, or even entire cases as this study suggests, this would translate into a significant reduction in the cost of a PBL curriculum. This may be of particular relevance where medical student numbers are increasing in the absence of commensurate funding.[12]

The most cost-effective approach to the implementation and maintenance of PBL in any particular medical school will depend on the staffing and organisational structure in place and the balance between research and teaching being undertaken by these staff members. Programmes that use existing academic staff will find that the costs of establishing and maintaining PBL are less than those programmes that employ casual tutors whose payments will need to be absorbed over and above what is already being paid in salaries to academic staff. Moreover, there will be significant and recurrent costs for training of casual tutors. High-quality, medically trained tutors will inevitably cost more. In a long-established school with a high proportion of active research staff, it is likely that casual tutors will predominate. In that case, there is a risk, unless teaching is adequately funded, that income from research and related activities such as supervision of postgraduate students will be used to cross subsidise teaching. Conversely, absorbing full-time academics into a largely PBL-based programme may erode time for research and creative activity.

Although more enjoyable and nurturing, there is no compelling evidence for improved learning or better outcomes overall from PBL compared with traditional curricula.[13,14,15] Epstein has drawn attention to particular concerns associated with PBL-based curricula, which include the patchy nature of knowledge acquired and the creation of an impression that a defined spectrum of core factual knowledge may suffice for clinical competence.[16] This may be considered a 'quality cost' and may be one reason why graduates of PBL programme have been found to have higher levels of self-confidence.[17,18] Epstein has also indicated that there may an 'improvement cost' because teachers are dissuaded from refining the educational utility of didactic modalities.[19] None of this means that the original ideology that underlays the implementation of PBL is flawed, and there are benefits associated with PBL for many, if not all, students. PBL during medical school appears to have particular benefits in the social and cognitive dimensions of clinical performance after graduation, although for the most part these seem to be modest.[20]

Nevertheless, PBL, at least as originally conceived, is probably not ideal as the sole or even predominant methodology for the delivery of a preclinical curriculum. McMaster Medical School has extensively revised its curriculum to a concept-based system, where emphasis is placed on underscoring the underlying concepts in the curriculum with a logical sequencing of both the concepts and the body systems.[21] For example, a conceptual theme might be oxygen supply and delivery. By studying problems around oxygen delivery, students acquire the necessary knowledge relating to the respiratory, cardiovascular and haematological systems. The curriculum is constructed in a web-based format and delivered electronically. Focused, shorter cases are used—allowing students to tackle important issues from more than one situation or clinical scenario. Expert tutors are used, and there is increased use of didactic sessions.[22]

We suggest that the following three principles need to be fulfilled in the construction of an optimal pedagogy and commensurate staffing establishment of a medical school in order for cost effectiveness to be optimised.

1 Medical students must graduate with a solid appreciation of the scientific basis (including the social and behavioural sciences) of contemporary medical practice and an understanding of how such evidence was generated. To this end, the importance of, and methodology for, critically evaluating evidence must be appreciated, and a passion and capacity for critical observation and perpetual enquiry instilled.

2 Medical education, rather than being an incidental activity undertaken by staff, must be organised academically, with a comprehensive programme of research, evaluation and quality assurance, and commensurate rewards. The ethos should be such that the value of ongoing enquiry and sharing of knowledge is perpetuated.

3 Integration of content should be paralleled by integration of expertise. It seems senseless to expect a PBL-based programme to function optimally when a traditional discipline-based structure is maintained. Rather a 'distributed model' is better—where teams are formed to deal with particular research themes and/or broad clinical areas. Such teams may variably comprise physician scientists/clinical academics, anatomists, molecular biologists, biochemists, epidemiologists and population health physicians as well as specialists in human behaviour and mental health, communication, ethics, nursing, rehabilitation, health systems and statistics. Such an environment will optimise both the research environment and the acquisition of the requisite knowledge, skills and attitudes, required for contemporary medical practice.

The most effective approach for achieving this is most likely to be that which optimises the benefits of PBL by combining it with clear learning objectives, case-based learning, elements of a didactic curriculum, such as mini-lectures, unbiased evaluation of student progress,[23,24,25] and making innovative use of online digital electronic resources (e-learning) and simulation for both purposes.

COMPLEMENTARY AND ALTERNATIVE APPROACHES TO OPTIMISE THE COST-EFFICACY OF PBL: E-LEARNING, SIMULATION AND RESOURCE SHARING

As an adjunct to face-to-face learning opportunities, the acquisition of knowledge and clinical problem-solving skills may be enhanced by e-learning, a medium that may also provide evaluation and feedback, and the opportunity to address areas of weakness contemporaneously.[26] Importantly, the medium facilitates the integration of basic, clinical and psychosocial concepts and provides considerable scope for interactive learning. For example, the creation of virtual patients by computer-based simulations may include basic science objectives; interpretation of symptoms, signs, laboratory and imaging data; simulation of the consequences of clinical decision-making; and training in cultural competency, chronic-disease management, care planning, patient-centred care and ethics.[27] In such a system, learning modules can be constructed that align with a curriculum map. For each learning module, the pre-requisite concepts and knowledge can be defined and assessed and opportunities for revision provided. The learning objectives for the module are made clear, and the student can undertake the activity without barriers of time or geography. The acquisition of the new knowledge may be subsequently assessed and feedback pro-vided to the student. The student in turn is able to provide feedback to the course coordinator. A system of this sort is also ideal to construct personalised learning portfolios for each student where they review their progress against the curricu-lum map, evaluate their knowledge and skill base as well as revise material where necessary. In addition, the electronic environment affords considerable opportu-nity for interactivity and group activity. Moreover, such systems have the capacity to accommodate different learning styles (e.g., by delivering material in both didactic and problem-based formats).[28] Interactive material can also be delivered via mobile devices thereby maximising convenience for students.[29]

At the University of Adelaide, a computing programme that uses a problem-solv-ing format has been shown to significantly increase the ophthalmology knowledge-base of students as well as stimulate further learning.[30] In Malawi, the introduction of, and engagement by teachers in, new approaches to medical education using elec-tronically delivered, personalised, context-sensitive content via a game-informed process has reduced staff teaching load, provided unique opportunities for collab-oration across universities, provided methods for coping with increasing student numbers, enhanced the creation of educational infrastructure and the promotion of professional development for teachers.[31]

Although the set-up cost may be considerable, this may be minimised by the for-mation of consortia among medical schools and sharing of resources, and the recur-rent costs are likely to be low, particularly if electronic curriculum management systems are used.[32] The case for a move towards the integration of computer-based learning in medical education is compelling although the optimal balance between methodologies remains uncertain.

LEARNING LABORATORIES AND TRAINED STANDARDISED PATIENTS

Although expensive to establish, the use of manikins and programmed simulation in a learning laboratory is an effective approach for the acquisition of basic clinical and basic examination skills,[33] and the integration of physiology and pathophysiology such as respiratory physiology and cardiovascular haemodynamics. In addition, it offers distinct educational advantages for learning how to recognise and treat complex, clinical problems, particularly those that are rare.[34] Advances in technology will inevitably result in increasingly lifelike manikins with sophisticated capabilities. In educating generations of students who will have had computer exposure since early childhood and are familiar and comfortable with simulation from gaming, a strong focus on this medium is now appropriate and arguably overdue. There is, however, no substitute for hands-on clinical experience with patients in clinical environments, and thus, the challenge remains in finding the appropriate balance, content and application for this educational tool.

Specially trained standardised patients can also effectively teach the normal physical examination to medical students and in addition facilitate the practice of communication skills; they are a less expensive alternative to traditional faculty small-group teaching methods.[35] In a programme run at the Geneva Medical School, patient-instructors have been shown to be valuable in developing the skills of students in important aspects of history taking and clinical examination in relation to rheumatoid arthritis as an example of a chronic inflammatory joint condition. Students are provided with direct constructive and didactic feedback from the patient-instructors on their approach and communication skills (empathy, politeness, appropriate information and listening).[36] Standardised patients have been used over the past several years at relatively low cost, in a highly rated programme, to teach rheumatology to medical students at the University of Adelaide (Prof L Cleland— Personal Communication).

CONCLUSIONS

In an evidence-based environment, the implementation of educational approaches without evidence of efficacy and cost is illogical. Innovative cost-constrained and effective programmes can be established. A recent example is a four-year curriculum emphasising comprehensive chronic-disease management and case-based and patient-centred education using collaborative, small-group and student learning communities.[37] The development and testing of innovative educational activities should be encouraged and fostered as an academic endeavour of high value,[38] with commensurate reward. An international platform for discussion and debate about curriculum design, pedagogy, methodology for evaluation and comparison of outcomes is required so that immediate and longer term outcomes and the costs associated with each approach can be assessed and meaningful comparisons made.

Such a forum may also facilitate innovation and, importantly in a cost-constrained environment, resource sharing. This may be accomplished by the creation of a virtual online community, a focussed agenda of regular round-table discussions, or both.

REFERENCES

1. Calvert MJ, Freemantle N. Cost-effective undergraduate medical education? *J R Soc Med.* 2009; **102**(2): 46–8.
2. Stark P, Fortune F. Teaching clinical skills in developing countries: are clinical skills centres the answer? *Educ Health (Abingdon).* 2003; **16**(3): 298–306.
3. Barrows H, Tamblyn R. *Problem-Based Learning: an approach to medical education.* New York, NY: Springer; 1980.
4. Elstein A, Shulman L, Sprafka S. *Medical Problem-Solving: an analysis of clinical reasoning.* Cambridge, MA: Harvard University Press; 1978.
5. Taylor D, Miflin B. Problem-based learning: where are we now? *Med Teach.* 2008; **30**(8): 742–63.
6. Barrows HS. A taxonomy of problem-based learning methods. *Med Educ.* 1986; **20**(6): 481–6.
7. Neufeld VR, Barrows HS. The "McMaster Philosophy": an approach to medical education. *J Med Educ.* 1974; **49**(11): 1040–50.
8. Wittert GA, Nelson AJ. Medical education: revolution, devolution and evolution in curriculum philosophy and design. *Med J Aust.* 2009; **191**(1): 35–7.
9. Finucane P, Shannon W, McGrath D. The financial costs of delivering problem-based learning in a new, graduate-entry medical programme. *Med Educ.* 2009; **43**(6): 594–8.
10. Zeitz HJ. Problem based learning: development of a new strategy for effective continuing medical education. *Allergy Asthma Proc.* 1999; **20**(5): 317–21.
11. Roberts C, Lawson M, Newble D, *et al.* The introduction of large class problem-based learning into an undergraduate medical curriculum: an evaluation. *Med Teach.* 2005; **27**(6): 527–33.
12. Parry J, Mathers J, Thomas H, *et al.* More students, less capacity? An assessment of the competing demands on academic medical staff. *Med Educ.* 2008; **42**(12): 1155–65.
13. Wittert, Nelson, op. cit.
14. Albanese MA, Mitchell S. Problem-based learning: a review of literature on its outcomes and implementation issues. *Acad Med.* 1993; **68**(1): 52–81.
15. Nandi PL, Chan JN, Chan CP, *et al.* Undergraduate medical education: comparison of problem-based learning and conventional teaching. *Hong Kong Med J.* 2000; **6**(3): 301–6.
16. Epstein RJ. Learning from the problems of problem-based learning. *BMC Med Educ.* 2004; **4**: 1.
17. Ibid.
18. Cohen-Schotanus J, Muijtjens AM, Schonrock-Adema J, *et al.* Effects of conventional and problem-based learning on clinical and general competencies and career development. *Med Educ.* 2008; **42**(3): 256–65.

19. Epstein, op. cit.
20. Koh GC, Khoo HE, Wong ML, *et al.* The effects of problem-based learning during medical school on physician competency: a systematic review. *CMAJ.* 2008; **178**(1): 34–41.
21. Neville AJ, Norman GR. PBL in the undergraduate MD program at McMaster University: three iterations in three decades. *Acad Med.* 2007; **82**(4): 370–4.
22. Ibid.
23. Wittert, Nelson, op. cit.
24. Nandi, Chan, Chan, *et al.* op. cit.
25. Lohfeld L, Neville A, Norman G. PBL in undergraduate medical education: a qualitative study of the views of Canadian residents. *Adv Health Sci Educ Theory Pract.* 2005; **10**(3): 189–214.
26. Devitt P, Palmer E. Computers in medical education 1: evaluation of a problem-orientated learning package. *Aust N Z J Surg.* 1998; **68**(4): 284–7.
27. Huang G, Reynolds R, Candler C. Virtual patient simulation at US and Canadian medical schools. *Acad Med.* 2007; **82**(5): 446–51.
28. Devitt P, Palmer E. Computer-aided learning: an overvalued educational resource? *Med Educ.* 1999; **33**(2): 136–9.
29. Palmer EJ, Devitt PG. A method for creating interactive content for the iPod, and its potential use as a learning tool: technical advances. *BMC Med Educ.* 2007; **7**: 32.
30. Devitt P, Smith JR, Palmer E. Improved student learning in ophthalmology with computer-aided instruction. *Eye (Lond).* 2001; **15**(Pt. 5): 635–9.
31. Dewhurst D, Borgstein E, Grant ME, *et al.* Online virtual patients – A driver for change in medical and healthcare professional education in developing countries? *Med Teach.* 2009; **31**(8): 721–4.
32. McGowan J, Abrams M, Frank M, *et al.* Creating a virtual community of learning predicated on medical student learning styles. *AMIA Annu Symp Proc.* 2003; 435–44.
33. Hao J, Estrada J, Tropez-Sims S. The clinical skills laboratory: a cost-effective venue for teaching clinical skills to third-year medical students. *Acad Med.* 2002; **77**(2): 152.
34. Good ML. Patient simulation for training basic and advanced clinical skills. *Med Educ.* 2003; **37**(Suppl. 1): 14–21.
35. Davidson R, Duerson M, Rathe R, *et al.* Using standardized patients as teachers: a concurrent controlled trial. *Acad Med.* 2001; **76**(8): 840–3.
36. Bideau M, Guerne PA, Bianchi MP, *et al.* Benefits of a programme taking advantage of patient-instructors to teach and assess musculoskeletal skills in medical students. *Ann Rheum Dis.* 2006; **65**(12): 1626–30.
37. Rackleff LZ, O'Connell MT, Warren DW, *et al.* Establishing a regional medical campus in southeast Florida: successes and challenges. *Acad Med.* 2007; **82**(4): 383–9.
38. Epstein, op. cit.

CHAPTER 10

Cost-benefit analysis of curriculum design for medicine

Rodney Gale and Janet Grant

A teacher's day is one-half bureaucracy, one-half crisis, one-half monotony, and one-eightieth epiphany. Never mind the arithmetic.

—Susan Ohanian

INTRODUCTION

Deciding on the wisdom of investing in a potential project has always required a little more than guesswork, and there are several related economic methods that have been developed to try to measure the benefit of a potential new project or new venture. Cost-benefit analysis is one such method, and it relies on it being possible to ascribe a precise monetary value to the various changes that would be wrought were the project to go ahead. It also requires the venture to be viewed as a project with reasonably well-defined boundaries; otherwise, the estimation of benefits and costs becomes much less precise because of intervening effects. Developing or modifying a curriculum could be viewed as a project, and it will have effects beyond its own boundaries.

A COST-BENEFIT MODEL

A number of models have emerged to take account of the financial and social nature of investment decisions across a broad spectrum of society. Sophisticated economic calculations have been developed but are not particularly useful to the practitioner trying to decide how much to spend on the new curriculum. Simpler methods are required.

Discounting

Projects have a life span, and yet there has to be a method of viewing future flows of cost and benefit in today's terms. Economists discount future income and expenditure (i.e., convert future values into present day values) at a rate that reflects the time value of money, which changes with inflation, and the inherent risks in the project. When the discounted values are summed, a net present value (NPV) is arrived at.[1] The NPV of optional investments provides a method to rank such investments and help choose between them. Discounting can be thought of as the inverse of compound interest on savings. If I save £1000, after 1 year it will be £110 at 10% interest. After 2 years, it will be worth £121, after 3 years £133.1, and so on. Discounting is the equivalent of saying, 'how much do I need to invest today to generate a given sum in the future?' A simple example follows.

Imagine a project where we spend £1000 and we get benefits of £400 in each of the next 3 years. This would appear to be a worthwhile project and increase our money. If we choose the 10% discount rate, purely for illustration, we get the following values (*see* Table 10.1).

A negative NPV implies we would be better off not investing in the project. If, however, we chose to discount at 6%, the NPV becomes positive (*see* Table 10.2).

The choice of a discount rate is a complex subject in itself. In financial terms, it is a reflection of the interest rates available from money markets combined with an inflation factor and a risk factor for the type of project. For the United Kingdom, a factor in the region of 5–6% is reasonable.

TABLE 10.1 Negative net present value

	Year 0	Year 1	Year 2	Year 3
Money flow	−1000	+400	+400	+400
Discount factor at 10% per year		1.1	1.21	1.331
Discounted value		363.6	330.6	300.5
NPV	−5.4			

TABLE 10.2 Positive net present value

	Year 0	Year 1	Year 2	Year 3
Money flow	−1000	+400	+400	+400
Discount factor at 6% per year		1.06	1.123	1.191
Discounted value		377.4	356.0	335.8
NPV	+69.2			

TABLE 10.3 Zero net present value

	Year 0	Year 1	Year 2	Year 3
Money flow	−1000	+400	+400	+400
Discount factor at 9.7% per year		1.097	1.203	1.32
Discounted value		364.6	332.4	303.0
NPV	0.0			

Rate of return

A variant of discounting methodology is to calculate the discount rate that will leave a zero NPV.[2] Some advocate choosing projects with the highest internal 'rate of return' as the calculated discount rate is called. Projects with the highest internal rate of return are preferred as investments. There are flaws in this method because the rates calculated are often outside the range that financial institutions might apply if lending the money and so provide an unreal valuation.

If we use the same money flows as before, the discount rate that gives a zero NPV is a fraction under 10% and is close to 9.7% (see Table 10.3).

Social cost benefit

Social cost-benefit analysis was developed to evaluate major infrastructure projects, such as river crossings, town bypasses or the creation of preschool nurseries, where the benefits are returned to society rather than to a single organisation.[3] The essence is to put a value on the social benefits, such as the shortened journey times for work and leisure, the increased safety of an upgraded road system or of the expanded provision of early education.[4] The expected life span of the scheme is important, as are the side effects of creating individuals with more disposable income. In education, particularly in the developing world, the costs and benefits are shared by the individual and society.[5]

Assessing the value of an extra year in education requires an estimation of the additional costs of the year to the individual and society, such as the wages given up and the taxes lost over the course of the working life. Societal benefits also arise from a more educated population; healthcare, diet and household management improves, all of which reduce burdens on society. Society bears the opportunity cost of providing the education premises and of organising the movement of money to fund education.

APPLICATION TO EDUCATION

Cost-benefit analysis applied to medical education[6] and the undergraduate curriculum, in particular, needs to consider three types of costs and benefits: direct, indirect and societal. The first two are felt by the organisation and its constituents, whereas the latter is felt in a much wider arc of society.

A direct cost is one that is intimately associated with a particular activity and would be avoided if that activity were not to take place. It can take the form of a financial expenditure, such as printing or a skills laboratory, or the use of internal resources such as the time of key staff and office space. A direct benefit is also something directly linked to an activity and dependent upon it. An example might be a course fee or the retention of a subsidy relating to places filled in a medical school.

Indirect costs have a broad impact on the supporting infrastructure of an institution. An increase in activity requires more human resources activity, more financial transactions and more institutional infrastructure. Working on a new curriculum takes up a lot of meeting space and squeezes out other uses of the space.

Societal costs and benefits are felt outside the institution. For example, medical students become doctors and influence healthcare, but society subsidises medical school training places and has to give up alternative investments to do so. Trained doctors have a significant effect on the economic productivity of those they treat and have disposable income that affects the economy around where they settle.

CURRICULUM DEFINITION: REVIEWING COSTS AND BENEFITS

When considering the costs and benefits of a well-designed and managed curriculum, we will use the UK Postgraduate Medical Education and Training Board definition.[7] A curriculum is a 'statement of the intended aims and objectives, content, experiences, outcomes and processes of an educational programme, including

- a description of the training structure (entry requirements, length and organisation of the programme including its flexibilities, and assessment system)
- a description of expected methods of learning, teaching, feedback and supervision.

The syllabus content of the curriculum should be stated in terms of what knowledge, skills, attitudes and expertise the learner will achieve'.

It can be seen from this that, in defining a curriculum, we are really describing a successful medical school.

A UK medical school typically has a fixed number of training places allocated and cannot reap the benefits of a well-crafted new curriculum in terms of fees from additional students. The benefits are felt as the avoidance of costs that might arise from a badly constructed curriculum.[8] These are mostly remedial costs for additional teaching, enhanced pastoral care and the need to redesign large chunks of the course that might arise from an inadequately designed or managed curriculum. There are potential costs arising from a loss of reputation, such as reduced research income, higher staff turnover or failing ability to attract the best faculty. These costs will vary with each school and each context in which it operates, and so it is really only practicable to identify the types of cost and quantify them approximately. This is even more the case, internationally, where different funding and competition regimes are in force. By thinking generically, it is possible to provide some useful insights with real numbers.

There are two clear ways to review curriculum costs and benefits. The first is to consider the essential stages in producing a new curriculum and to discuss the resource implications of each stage. The second is to look at the consequences of a dysfunctional curriculum in terms of the remedial actions, reputational consequences and impacts of substandard patient care that follow.

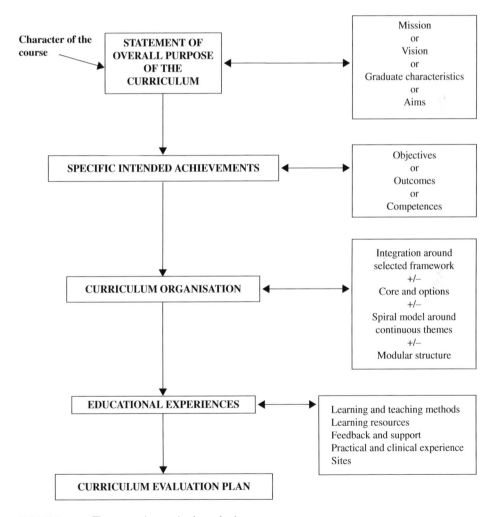

FIGURE 10.1 The steps in curriculum design

CURRICULUM DESIGN STAGES

Figure 10.1 shows the steps in curriculum design. Purely for the purposes of illustration, we will assume that the curriculum takes a whole year to develop and will last for a further 5 years. In reality, development may take considerably longer. As we work down through the design steps, the number of people involved and the effort needed increase quite rapidly.

THE COSTS OF CURRICULUM DESIGN BY STAGE

Development stage

We assume a medical education department of three people involved full time with administrative backup of two further people. There will almost certainly be a steering group of about five moderately senior people who spend 20% of their time in meetings and reviewing draft documentation. This amounts to a full-time senior academic.

The preliminary stages of deciding the purpose and expected outcomes of the curriculum involve a large volume of consultations and explanatory meetings with associated costs, such as the time commitments of the participants in preparing for and attending meetings and the time and material costs of producing documents for review. Wide consultation is an important investment that is repaid in a smoother process of creating the contents of the curriculum. Some people will spend a lot of time on this stage and others a matter of a few days. The total effort could be the equivalent of one academic, full time for the year. There will be indirect effects on the administrative support function and on the communications department who will have more of their discretionary time diverted to the cause of the new curriculum at a cost of diluting their attention to other matters. If the curriculum is a radical departure from the existing version, then extra time and effort may well be required to convince a critical mass of academics in order to proceed.

Organising the curriculum

Once we reach the stage of organising the curriculum and fashioning the student experience, every department will need dedicated staff to ensure a balanced curriculum and integrated student experiences through teaching modes, teaching materials and assessment methods. The more radical the curriculum, the more the effort needed. It is easy to envisage the discussion, the reports, the meetings, the drafts, the amendments, more meetings and so on. It is not unreasonable to estimate that 10 departments will put in the equivalent of 6 months work. This amounts to five person-years of academic input. There will be other direct costs associated with purchase and production of a variety of teaching materials. Coordination and organisation of this production effort constitutes a large indirect cost, and the large number of meetings will put pressure on the meeting facilities. Labour-intensive curricula may need more staff time, and technology-based approaches may generate more costs.

Running the curriculum

There is a further set of costs to consider in relation to managing the new curriculum into place. All staff will need to be informed of their roles and duties, and some will need to be trained in new methods. A large number of prospectuses will need to be produced and distributed and, possibly, explained. Students need to learn their way around the curriculum, too. In the first run of the new curriculum, there will be some adjustments to contents and running orders and revisions of some training materials, but careful design work should help to minimise this cost. The more radical the design, the more one would envisage difficulties. Maintenance and improvement work in year two should be less than in year one but may rise again towards the end of the useful life of the curriculum. The level of remedial work on the curriculum may actually provide a leading indicator of the need for a complete redesign.

The medical education department will continue to be engaged in this stage of development, and the three team members will work full time. The assessment committee will have a heavy workload to map assessment onto the curriculum and ensure that it is fit for purpose and offers valid and reliable results. Each of 10 departments will have the equivalent of a person working for 20% of her or his time on curriculum matters, and there will be a management committee of about 12 members preparing and meeting monthly for 4 hours. The academic input could amount to the equivalent of two full-time staff, and the management and assessment committees will add nearly another half-year to the total, in the first year of operation. This expenditure would continue for the life of the curriculum, at a reduced level, probably, in years two and three, but rising again in year four as the curriculum matures and needs more revision. It is possible that some forms of teaching and learning may require additional investment in new, or altered, teaching space, in addition to the production costs.

This pattern of expenditure is purely indicative and illustrative and serves to raise the topics that will vary with the circumstances of each medical school.

Evaluation plan

The evaluation plan for the curriculum will take account of the novelty of the curriculum and the degree of experimentation with the mix of teaching and learning methods. All change, even if seemingly minor, should be evaluated to ensure that it meets the desired purpose.[9] There might be a need for modified data gathering methods and more elaborate evaluation events. New curricula also generate added academic activity. Clearly, minor changes can be evaluated moderately quickly and at low cost. The hopes of curriculum designers are not always delivered in practice.

The medical education team will be the main internal cost concerning evaluation, but due consideration needs to be given to employing independent evaluators, particularly in the case of experimental elements of the curriculum or the adoption of teaching and learning methods developed in disciplines other than medicine. This cost could amount to the equivalent of employing an additional academic for a whole year, possibly more.

In summary, the costs of each stage of the development of the new curriculum are recorded in Table 10.4.

THE BENEFITS AND COSTS OF THE CONSEQUENCES OF CURRICULUM DESIGN

While a good curriculum should produce effective doctors, the benefits of investing properly in curriculum development and management reside mostly in the avoidance of additional remedial costs or avoidance of the consequences of diminished reputation or standing in the academic and research communities, or the avoidance of the effects of poorly trained doctors. Some of these benefits are hard to quantify precisely but can have a major impact. For example, loss of research income, either absolute or relative to others, can be very damaging. Equally important is loss of overall reputation such that excellent faculty are not attracted to join the institution, or the existing faculty seek opportunities elsewhere. The consequences of insufficient investment in curriculum design are analysed below in terms of direct, indirect and societal costs that arise from poor design and management of curriculum. Each section is based around the characteristics of a well-designed and managed curriculum.

The medical school attracts the most appropriate recruits to its places

Clarity about the purpose, structure and components of the curriculum ensures that students who are attracted to it share its values and approach to learning. Failure to attract the most appropriate students has a direct impact, in that extra teaching effort will be needed to compensate and maintain the output quality. Extra tutorial support may be necessary, and it is likely that student concerns will be raised and effort will be required to ameliorate the situation. It may be necessary to recruit more faculty or to divert their time from research and scholarship.

Indirect consequences may be felt in the need for enhanced pastoral support of students and the office functions that keep track of progress. There may be human resource costs, too.

The social costs of a cohort of medical students who underperform are felt further down the career path when postgraduate trainers and educational supervisors may have to invest their time in remedial training. In severe form, there may not be enough recruits of sufficient calibre to meet the needs of the healthcare system without additional supervision and remedial training.

The students cope with the pace and volume of work and thrive

The curriculum design is such that students are stretched but not overwhelmed and gain confidence as they progress. Poor design of curriculum may manifest itself in underperformance and dissatisfied students rather than in the manner of inappropriate selection. The direct and indirect costs of remedial action are also similar, as are societal costs.

The components of the course dovetail well

Good curriculum design ensures that the component parts dovetail together and the interfaces work well. Harmony is maintained between the various departments and faculty, and all share responsibility for the curriculum. If the planning has not been sufficiently profound, the parts will grate against each other, and remedial interventions will be required.

There could be profound societal effects on the institution's health if some departments come to apportion blame for shortcomings to particular people or groups of faculty. This can have a negative effect on the overall performance of the institution as energies are directed to inward battles.

Everyone understands the educational process

A further attribute of good curriculum design is that the faculty and students understand how they are expected to attain the knowledge and skill required to obtain their qualifications. Everyone is clear about the roles played by various departments and particular teachers. Everyone understands how to access supporting materials and human support. Everyone understands the assessment system. There is the minimum need for redesign and corrective interventions.

The converse may well result in underperformance and generate consequences for the institution through a loss of reputation and the production of doctors lacking all the attributes necessary to lead the profession in the future. If the underperformance is spotted early enough, then remedial action will represent a further cost that good curriculum design could avoid.

The students acquire the appropriate knowledge to practise medicine

The frame of reference needs to be set very broadly, so that we examine the quality of the product of the course and do not just count the numbers who pass or fail. The curriculum may be internally consistent but it still has to produce graduates that fit into the healthcare system.

The costs of failure in this regard fall mostly outside the institution in that other organisations bear the cost of remedial training or the costs of inadequate clinical performance. There are reputational costs to consider, which may impact on the overall standing of the institution.

The graduates are able to secure places in the better clinical training programmes

The vast majority of medical graduates are expected to go on and practise medicine. Each jurisdiction has its own routes to practice, and there are always perceptions that career progression or access to particular career niches are influenced by the training pathway that is available. A well-designed and appropriate curriculum that generates graduates with appropriate skills and attributes will enable the graduates to gain places on the better clinical training programmes. Success in this aspect builds reputation, particularly among potential students so that the more able are attracted to the course.

The consequences of inadequate attention to this detail are mostly felt by society which runs the risk of its doctors not delivering to their full potential because they have not gained access to the career niches they could perhaps have attained. This equates to a diminished return on society's investment in supporting medical schools and meeting the costs of training medical students. For example, this might be particularly the case where curricula are designed to attract graduates to practise in rural or community settings.

The institution attracts and retains the highest calibre staff

The cost effectiveness of medical training depends on having teaching staff of high calibre, and the medical school relies on continuing to attract research funding. A good curriculum can attract new faculty and help retain existing high calibre staff. They should be able to devote time to research and scholarship, because the curriculum is running smoothly.

An inability to attract and retain the highest calibre staff means that they go to a competitor institution. The teaching staff have a large impact on the perceived quality of the curriculum, and diminished status may affect the calibre of student applicants. In privately run medical schools, this may adversely affect income. If staff, in any school, are having to spend a larger proportion of their time in delivering the curriculum, they will inevitably be spending less on research and scholarship and will contribute less to the challenge of generating research income.

The medical school always passes external inspections

The external regulation of medical schools is an important part of the process of assuring quality of output. A well-designed and managed curriculum can be scrutinised at any time and meet the regulatory requirements. A medical school with a less well-designed and managed curriculum will have to invest considerable time and effort in readying itself to face a regulatory visit.

The consequences of finding one's institution on the wrong side of the acceptable level of performance can be quite profound and will trigger the need for investment in changes to satisfy the regulators and overcome the reputational damage. In extreme cases, the allocation of training places could be put in jeopardy.

The school's graduates go on to practise safe medicine

The medical school is early in the chain that leads to a doctor in practice, but the aim of producing doctors who are capable of practising safe and cost-effective medicine must be present, whether through the knowledge imparted or the professional attitudes that are instilled.

The costs of deficient medical training are felt by society at large in the form of inadequate patient care, in the guise of poor diagnostic behaviour and in higher rates of treatment error. Hospitals and primary care organisations may bear the costs of such inadequacy through diminished efficiency and increased litigation.

DISCUSSION

The variety of medical schools and the variety of curriculum models with differing intensities of faculty involvement, make exact quantification almost impossible, even for the direct and indirect costs and benefits that are felt at the institutional level. To use cost-benefit analysis as a precise decision tool would require attention to calculating the costs of inadequacies in curriculum design to the broader society of the medical school and to the healthcare systems themselves. This is not a trivial task, and the challenge of correctly attributing failures in performance to failures in teaching, when there have been a number of intervening activities from outside bodies, is far from trivial. Subjecting one's plans to the discipline of cost-benefit analysis, albeit suffused with approximations and estimations can, however, provide some sort of framework to help decide how much effort needs to be put into proper curriculum design and management.

Within the curriculum, it is possible to use cost-benefit analysis to illuminate the consequences of particular choices of curriculum style. An integrated curriculum based around organs or systems may play down the autonomy of some of the specialist departments, such as pathology or biochemistry, and tend to diminish their contributions. A problem-based curriculum may require more effort in the selection and preparation of cases and in the student support required.

Table 10.4 may be helpful in considering the costs and benefits germane to a particular situation. They are deliberately illustrative rather than comprehensive in the topics listed and costed. Benefits are shown as positive numbers and costs as negative (*see* Table 10.4).

In this case, a positive NPV indicates that the benefits of investing in the curriculum outweigh the costs of proper design and implementation.

TABLE 10.4 The costs of the development of a curriculum

Activity	Year 0	Year 1	Year 2	Year 3	Year 4	Year 5
Costs incurred*						
Consultation on design: 3 × educationalist, 2 × administrator, 2 × academic + 5× academic	−£940k					
Running the curriculum: 3 × educationalist, 2 × administrator, variable academic		−£490k	−£340k	−£340k	−£390k	−£440k
Evaluation, external costs		−£100k	−£50k	−£50k		
Indirect cost estimate	−£100k	−£50k	−£50k	−£50k	−£50k	−£50k
Material cost estimate	−£100k	−£50k	−£20k	−£30k	−£50k	−£50k
Benefits delivered						
Remedial action avoided: saving 3 × academic		£300k	£300k	£300k	£300k	£300k
Student income retained		£100k	£100k	£100k	£100k	£100k
Research income retained		£500k	£500k	£500k	£500k	£500k
The sum of all transactions in each column	−£1140k	£210k	£440k	£430k	£410k	£360k
Discount factors at 10%	1	1.1	1.21	1.331	1.4641	1.612
Present value = sum of transactions/discount factor	−1140k	£191k	£393k	£323k	£280k	£224k
NPV = sum of present values	£271k					

*Educationalists cost £60 000, administrators £30,000 and clinical academics £100 000.

REFERENCES

1. Franks J, Broyles JE. *Modern Managerial Finance.* Chichester: Wiley; 1979; Campbell HF. *Benefit Cost Analysis: financial and economic appraisal using spreadsheets.* Cambridge: Cambridge University Press, 2003.
2. Ibid.
3. Mishen EJ, Quah E. *Cost Benefit Analysis.* 5th ed. Abingdon, Oxon: Routledge; 2007.
4. Woodhall M. *Cost Benefit Analysis in Educational Planning.* 4th ed. Paris: UNESCO, 2004.
5. Sevick MA. Cost effectiveness of lifestyle and structured exercise interventions in sedentary adults. *Am J Prevent Med.* 2000; **19**(1): 1–6; Jimenez E, Patrinos HA. Can cost-benefit analysis guide education policy in developing countries? Policy Research Working Paper 4568. The World Bank; 2008. Available at: www.econ. queensu.ca/faculty/kuog/references/D10+D11+Patrinos_Education_2004.pdf (accessed June 2010).
6. Hough JR. Educational cost benefit analysis. *Educ Econ.* 1994; **2**(2): 93–128
7. Grant JR. Principles of curriculum design. In: *Understanding Medical Education (monograph series).* Edinburgh: ASME, 2006.
8. Masse LN, Barnet WS. A benefit cost analysis of the Abecedarian early childhood interventions. *Econ Educ Rev.* 2007; **26**(3): 395–6.
9. Grant JR, Gale R. Managing change in a medical context: guidelines for action (AMEE Education Guides No. 10). *Med Teach.* 1997; **19**(4): 239–49.

CHAPTER 11

Cost-effective assessment

Lambert Schuwirth and Cees van der Vleuten

There is no end to education. It is not that you read a book, pass an examination, and finish with education. The whole of life, from the moment you are born to the moment you die, is a process of learning.

—*Jiddu Krishnamurti*

INTRODUCTION

Cost-effective assessment nowadays seems like a contradiction in terms. In an era in which all kinds of new and resource-intensive methods are developed and introduced in practice, it seems almost hilarious to talk about cost effectiveness. Granted, in modern education, emphasis is increasingly placed not only on the quality of assessment but also on the shift from assessment *of* learning to assessment *for* learning. The implications of this are huge. Instead of using assessment merely for the purpose of determining whether the candidate has learnt enough, modern assessment is designed to inform the student about his or her progress, to give detailed feedback as to specific strengths and weaknesses and how to remediate the latter, to provide the faculty with information as to the efficacy of the curriculum and to satisfy the increased demand from society for evidence of the quality of the graduated doctors. It is only logical that such increased demands and wide array of purposes ask for more investments in assessment. This, however, should never lead to unnecessary spending of resources in assessment. Despite the increased demands, assessment should always be set up to achieve the maximum result with efficient effort. The purpose of this chapter is to highlight sources of ineffective assessment procedures and to provide suggestions for how to avoid them. This being said, cheaper is, of course, not always better, and to determine whether an assessment approach is cost-effective, it should be weighed against other qualities. The most often used qualities are reliability, validity, educational impact and acceptability.

Reliability indicates the extent to which a score or decision generalises to the score that a candidate would obtain if he or she were presented with all the possible relevant questions or tasks of a certain discipline. In other words, if someone scores 58% on an internal medicine test, does this mean that he or she would score 58% on a test containing all possible relevant internal medicine questions? It seems like an impossible question to answer, and a detailed explanation of the underlying concepts and statistics fall beyond the scope of this chapter. It may suffice to realise that any test is a sample from the whole domain or population of possible questions. In statistical testing, a similar problem exists, namely to infer significance from the composition of the sample. In a similar way, reliability can be estimated from the sample of items in a test. For normal use, reliability is a rather straightforward concept. It ranges from 0 to 1, and the closer it is to 1 the better the reliability is.

Validity relates to the extent to which the test actually measures what it purports to measure. This may seem simple, but one has to keep in mind that many of the things we try to assess are not directly visible. For example, problem-solving ability is not directly visible, but it has to be inferred from multiple observations of someone solving medical problems. There are mainly two approaches to validity. The so-called indirect validity is based on the 'behaviour' of the scores, by determining whether experts score higher on the test than novices. The other sort of validity—direct validity—aims at making sure the items on a test are well-written, well-selected and relevant and that the test forms a good stratified sample from the whole domain. So, in the former case, validity has to be established by statistical analyses and, in the latter, validity has to be built into the test by careful item construction, item review and blueprinting. The latter must be seen as a stratification of the sample. Before the test is constructed, a matrix is constructed clearly defining how many items are asked on each subject. This is done to improve the content validity of the test.

Educational impact refers to all consequences a test or assessment programme has on the way teachers teach and test on the one hand and on how students learn on the other. For example, if the organisation prescribes a multiple-choice format, teachers often test things that can easily be asked in such a format, and they neglect aspects that are more difficult to cast in that way. Students are often chided for being so assessment driven, but, basically, it is only human to aim for those factors that determine success. Ideally, the assessment would be designed such that learning for the assessment would be the same as learning to become a better doctor. Unfortunately, assessment often rewards other aspects (e.g., cramming behaviour). It is logical that students will adapt their behaviour to the assessment, because this is what defines academic success. Finally, acceptability is an essential assessment quality. An assessment that is great on all other aspects but that is undoable or completely unacceptable to the users will not 'survive' for long. A good assessment procedure therefore has to be acceptable.

EXAMPLES OF COST-INEFFECTIVENESS
Belief in expensive methods

Quite a large array of different assessment methods in medical education have been developed (each with its own acronym) and presented in the medical education literature. It is only logical that the authors who present a new method that they have developed themselves are perhaps slightly over-enthusiastic about the added value their instrument has to the existing armamentarium. Often new methods are heralded as the solution to all assessment problems. Extensive research in the past four decades, however, has provided us with some robust insights about these added values. One of the most robust findings is that in matters of validity (i.e., the type of competence an assessment method assesses), the content of the test is far more important than its format.[1,2] In other words, what the assessment asks the candidates to do is far more important than how the answers are collected. For example, there is a large set of studies comparing open-ended with multiple-choice questions, and the outcome of the large majority is that when the content of the questions is similar in both formats, the differences are negligible. Often, mean scores on the open-ended set are somewhat lower, but true (corrected for unreliability) correlations often approach unity. Important in the interpretation of these findings is that the comparisons were made with both formats asking the same content. The reverse is not true; not all contents can be asked in any format. Obviously, questions asking for creative aspects, such as hypothesis generation, relationships between concepts and spontaneous on-spot diagnoses, cannot be cast successfully into a multiple-choice format. On the other hand, questions to which there are only a limited number of realistic answers should not be asked with open-ended questions. The guiding principle in this matter should therefore be to let the content of the assessment determine the format and not the other way around.

Typical examples of cost-inefficient uses in assessment are the use of expensive open-ended or oral assessments, where a written multiple-choice type would be equally valid.

In this time of increasing computer use, it is also important to realise that computerised assessment is not always an improvement over paper-and-pencil assessment. A careful consideration of all the costs involved in computerised assessment should be considered and weighed against the costs of a paper-and-pencil test administration. The costs associated with the purchase or development of the software, the licence costs, the write-off of the infrastructure (e.g., computers or network facilities) and the time of the systems administrator can be considerable compared with the costs of paper reproduction, even if this entails glossy photo prints. And, finally, one has to remember that it is the content of the assessment that is essential and not the presentation format, so a multiple-choice test on a computer is just a multiple-choice test.

Inefficient sampling

In the previous paragraphs, it was explained that sampling is essential in achieving sufficient or high reliability. It is therefore important to set up the assessment so that a maximum reliability per hour of testing time can be achieved most efficiently. A number of examples can be used to demonstrate this.

When correcting an essay test, different approaches can be taken. Assume that a test containing five long essay questions is administered to 300 students, and there are five markers to correct them. One approach is to subdivide the workload amongst the markers by students, so marker 1 would correct the complete papers of the first 60 students, marker 2 the next set of 60 students, and so on. Another approach is to subdivide the workload by questions, so marker 1 would correct the first essay question for all students, marker 2 would correct question number 2 for all students, etc. The latter approach is far more efficient than the former. Not only will the markers more quickly 'get a feel' for the correct and incorrect answers, and they will have to go back to previously marked essays less frequently, but more importantly the total score of each student is now based on the marking of five markers. As the marker is a factor in unreliability (e.g., because of their differences in stringency), a sample of five is more reliable than a sample of only one. So, not only will the total marking time decrease but also the result of this marking scheme will be more reliable.

Another frequently made mistake is to use two examiners in an objective-structured clinical examination. It may seem more objective to have two examiners per station, but, in fact, the added value of the second in terms of reliability is quite limited. Some studies have shown that the inter-examiner agreement within a station is high, and so the added value of an extra examiner within a station is very limited. Studies estimating reliabilities comparing objective-structured clinical examinations (OSCEs) with fewer and more stations and comparing OSCEs with one and two examiners per station show that adding stations increases reliability considerably, whereas adding examiners has a negligible effect.[3]

Unnecessary long observations

In assessment, the law of diminishing returns often plays an important role. For good validity and reliability of an assessment, it is imperative that good content sampling takes place. For this, it is essential to have sufficient variety of items, cases or assignments. For summative purposes, it may not always be efficient to rely on long cases or long observations in practice. Much of the understanding of this has its origins in the research on long simulations in the 1970s and 1980s. In that period, long-branched case scenarios were extremely popular for the assessment of clinical problem-solving, the so-called patient management problems (PMPs).[4] These were developed under the impression that the higher the fidelity of the assessment procedure, the better its validity would be. Research in that area, however, soon showed some serious drawbacks of this approach (for an overview *see* Swanson,

Norcini and Grosso[5]). First, it was repeatedly found that experts who were asked to design a scoring rubric for all the possible decisions during the problem-solving process seldom agreed on the correct pathway through the simulation. Second, it was found that the problem-solving process was highly domain specific, meaning that how a candidate solved a certain case was an extremely poor predictor for how he or she would solve any other given case, even within the same domain. So, large numbers of cases, with extremely long testing times, were needed to come to reliable decision. These findings, along with the finding that the results correlated highly with straightforward knowledge-based multiple-choice questions, were the main reason why almost all of the major certification institutes have abandoned the long simulations. Currently, short case-based assessment is being used with more success, typical examples of which are the key-feature cases and the extended matching questions.[6,7] Key feature approach cases are short cases based on real authentic patient cases to which a limited number of questions (usually one to five) are posed, asking for essential decisions only. Extended-matching items are series of related short-case vignettes, each with the same set of options (e.g., diagnoses). For each vignette, the candidate has to indicate the most likely answer (e.g., the most likely diagnosis). Both methods have in common that the cases are kept short and that the questions are aimed at essential decisions. Therefore, for summative purposes, it is better to use a sample consisting of many short cases and/or observations than a few long ones.

Too many resit possibilities

There are quite a few downsides to allowing for multiple resit possibilities. In general, they are expensive tests, in that they need to be of high quality (as the stakes are high) but are often created for only a small group of students. Furthermore, resits are only useful if they are held after a period of serious remediation of the students. A resit without remediation is only capitalising on chance. This may need some explaining: with any test, some of the students will pass despite being not sufficiently competent (they could be considered false positives) and some will fail despite good competence (false negatives). Since only the failing students have to do the resits, the false positives will not be tested again. The failing students (both the true and the false negatives) will be tested again and will have another chance of passing purely by chance. If there has been no serious remediation, it is more likely that most of those who pass are false positives. Finally, many resit possibilities induce a minimalistic study strategy (there is always the extra resit possibility), which leads to more study delay. So, on the one hand, offering resit possibilities is fair to the students, but at the same time it is a cost-inefficient part of assessment. Generally, the best approach is to design resits in such a way that they become unattractive to students (e.g., scheduled during summer holidays) and that they allow ample opportunity for students to remediate.

Not-invented-here syndrome

This is definitely the most serious source of cost-ineffectiveness. All teachers at all schools have their personal 'drawers' with test questions. This seems strange because most medical curricula have similar courses, so it would be logical to share test material. Yet this does not happen on a large scale. There are some initiatives in producing joint item banks, such as the International Database for Enhanced Assessments and Learning (IDEAL consortium) (www.hkwebmed.org/idealweb/homeindex. html, accessed 19 October 2009), the Universities Medical Assessment Partnership (UMAP) project in the United Kingdom (www.umap.org.uk/) and the interuniversity progress test collaboration in the Netherlands.[8] The lack of collaboration is not only confined to assessment content but also to infrastructure. Many different institutes all have their custom-made software for item banking, item analysis and/ or test administration.

It must be said, however, that although it may seem a slightly ludicrous situation from a distance, collaboration is not easy. In some countries, there is competition between medical schools for the best students. This is not a sound basis for open sharing of material. In addition, not much is published and therefore known about the specific intricacies of such collaborations. One issue is the aspect of quality for quality. In a joint item bank project, procedures must be in place to ensure that the quality of the items of each contributor is at least equal to the quality of the items this contributor takes from the item bank. Whenever there is doubt or dispute over the quality of the items from one of the contributors, things rapidly become very complicated. Another issue is the academic culture. In some countries, it is perfectly normal to draw up legally valid contracts, regulating production and quality assurance so that if one of the partners fails to hold up to his or her obligations, another partner can pursue legal action enforce sanctions (e.g., financial claims). However, there are many cultures in which such an approach would simply not be considered.

Despite these and other hurdles, we would advocate whenever possible to collaborate on test production, item banking and sharing of infrastructure. The gains can be enormous. The participation of our medical school in the inter-university progress test collaboration has dropped the necessary resources (e.g., in teacher time) from 3.86 full-time equivalent to 1.66 full-time equivalent, and yet we were able to achieve an increase in quality of the assessment.

CONCLUSIONS

In this chapter, we have highlighted some of the major sources of cost-ineffective practices in assessment. We have only been able to describe the five most important— and most assessment-technical—aspects, but, of course, there are many more. For example, a lot is to be gained by a well-established organisation in which subject matter expert teachers are well supported by administrative and psychometric staff, in which there is a good information technology infrastructure with good item banking to guide an efficient reuse of items. These issues, though, are often self-evident. The more technical issues, especially those related to psychometric properties of assessment, may be less clear which is why we chose to focus this chapter on such issues.

REFERENCES

1. Norman G, Swanson D, Case S. Conceptual and methodology issues in studies comparing assessment formats, issues in comparing item formats. *Teach Learn Med.* 1996; 8(4): 208–16.
2. Ward WC. A comparison of free-response and multiple-choice forms of verbal aptitude tests. *Appl Psychol Measure.* 1982; 6(1): 1–11.
3. Van der Vleuten CPM, Swanson D. Assessment of clinical skills with standardized patients: state of the art. *Teach Learn Med.* 1990; 2(2): 58–76.
4. Berner ES, Hamilton LA, Best WR. A new approach to evaluating problem-solving in medical students. *J Med Educ.* 1974; 49: 666–72.
5. Swanson DB, Norcini JJ, Grosso LJ. Assessment of clinical competence: written and computer-based simulations. *Assess Eval Higher Educ.* 1987; 12(3): 220–46.
6. Page G, Bordage G, Allen T. Developing key-feature problems and examinations to assess clinical decision-making skills. *Acad Med.* 1995; 70(3): 194–201.
7. Case SM, Swanson DB. Extended-matching items: a practical alternative to free response questions. *Teach Learn Med.* 1993; 5(2): 107–115.
8. Muijtjens AMM, Schuwirth LWT, Cohen-Schotanus J, *et al.* Benchmarking by cross-institutional comparison of student achievement in a progress test. *Med Educ.* 2008; 42(1): 82–8.

CHAPTER 12

Cost-effective educational evaluation

John Goldie

If you have two pence to spend, you should spend a penny on bread and a penny on a flower, the bread to make life possible, the flower to make it worthwhile.

—Confucius

WHAT IS EVALUATION?

In education, the term evaluation is often used interchangeably with assessment, particularly in North America. Assessment is primarily concerned with the measurement of student performance, whereas evaluation is generally understood to refer to the process of obtaining information about an educational programme for subsequent judgment and decision-making. Evaluations can involve measuring student performance as a source of information, although it requires student testing both pre- and post-course. It must be remembered that, although evaluation may identify strengths and weaknesses, it cannot correct problems. This is in the hands of management and other stakeholders.

Early evaluators believed in the power of evaluation to transform poor educational programmes into highly effective ones and of the importance of evaluation results to decision-makers. However, experience has shown that most educational decisions of importance continued to be taken in a political, interpersonal milieu, where evidence plays a minor role.[1] Educational decision-makers typically made their choices without waiting for the 'definitive' results of evaluations (results which could be inconclusive). However, evaluators recognised that even though some attempts at evaluation did not work at all, others led to varying degrees of improvement. Improvement, even when modest, is valuable. Realising the political

101

nature of the decision-making process, educational evaluators began to embrace Cronbach's[2] view of evaluators as educators, in that they should rarely attempt to focus their efforts on satisfying a single decision-maker but on 'informing the relevant political community'.

WHAT IS BEST PRACTICE IN EVALUATION?

Initiation/commissioning

The initial stage of evaluation is where the institutions or individuals responsible for a programme take the decision to evaluate it. Evaluation should be considered at the planning stage and not left until the programme is up and running. Ideally, it should be part of an ongoing cycle of improvement (*see* Figure 12.1).

Activities that may be evaluated include the work undertaken by a teacher with his or her students, a curriculum or postgraduate course, an entire curriculum or even national programmes. Initiators must decide on the purpose of the evaluation and who will be responsible for undertaking it. Muraskin[3] lists some of the common reasons for undertaking evaluation:
- to determine the effectiveness of the programme for participants
- to document that the teaching objectives have been met

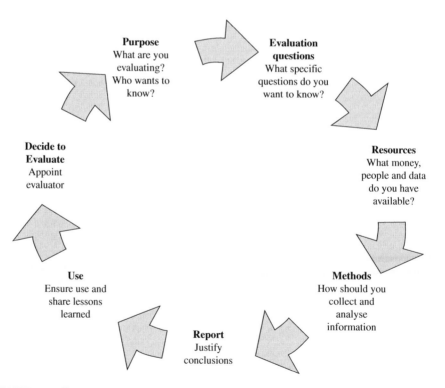

FIGURE 12.1 Best practice in evaluation

- to provide information about service delivery that will be useful to teachers and other audiences
- to enable changes to be made that improve the programme's effectiveness.

The potential cost of the evaluation often plays a major role in determining the scope of the evaluation as the cost will have to be met from the programme budget or by seeking additional funding. The question of whether the evaluator should be internal or external to the programme's development and delivery is considered at this point. Producing an effective educational evaluation may require skills from many disciplines, for example, psychology, sociology, philosophy, statistics, politics and economics. It is unlikely that one individual would have the competence to perform all these tasks or that an institution would have all these skills in-house.[4]

Defining the evaluator's role

Evaluation is an inherently value-laden activity. The evaluator(s), having been appointed, must reflect on their role. This will influence the decision-making process on the goals of the evaluation and the methodology to be used. It is at this point that the evaluator decides where, and to whom, his or her responsibility lies, and on the values to be made explicit. The questions listed in Box 12.1 may assist the evaluator.

Designing the evaluation

Having decided what needs to be done, the evaluator has to design an appropriate plan to obtain the relevant data. An important dimension to consider is whether the evaluation is to be formative or summative. Formative evaluation is undertaken during the course of a programme with a view to adjusting the materials or activities as the programme proceeds. Summative evaluation is carried out at the end. In the case of an innovative programme, it may be difficult to determine when the end has been reached, and often the length of time allowed before evaluation takes place will depend on the nature of the change.

Another important dimension to consider is whether to focus on process, outcome or impact information, or a mixture of all three. Process information is sought on the effectiveness of course materials and activities. Often the materials are examined during both development and implementation. Examination of the implementation of the programme documents what actually happens, and how closely it resembles the stated goals. This information can also be of use in studying outcomes. Outcome information can focus on the short-term or direct effects on participants. The effects on students' learning can be categorised as instructional (e.g., does the programme result in students being able to pass exams?) or nurturant (e.g., does it make a definite change in their personal development?). The method of obtaining information on the effects of learning will depend on which category

Box 12.1 Questions for the evaluator

Purpose

Why is the evaluation being initiated? What purposes might the evaluation serve? To measure the effects of the programme? To improve the programme? To influence the decision-makers? To judge its worth? To provide useful information? To explain how an intervention or ones like it, work? Why? How will you choose among these purposes?

Can you do all this within time and budget? If not, then what has the highest priority and why?

What are your fallback options if something goes wrong with any of these matters?

Cost-Benefit

Could the money earmarked for evaluation be better spent? Is it worth spending time and money on this evaluation given other things one could do? Why?

Evaluator's Role

What role do you want to play in the evaluation? Methodological expert? Servant to the management or some larger set of stakeholders? Judge of the programme's worth? Contributor to improvement? Servant of the 'public interest'? Educator of the client funding the evaluation? Why?

Data/Scope/Questions to be answered

What questions need to be answered by this evaluation? Where could you get the questions? From students, teachers, other stakeholders or those who paid for the evaluation? From past research, theory or evaluations? From pending decisions or legislation? Why?

Will you ask questions about real and potential students and their characteristics and needs? About how the programme is implemented? About student outcome, and impact on those with whom the students interact? About the connections among students, programme implementation and outcome? About costs and fiscal benefits? Why?

Methodology

What methods will you use? Why? Will these methods provide good answers to the questions you are asking? How will you measure programme performance?

Results

How do you plan to facilitate the use of the evaluation? Is it your responsibility to do so? Why? How should the results be communicated? Should interim results be reported periodically to users? In the final report, should you include an executive summary? Action recommendations? Should oral briefings be used? Should reports of evaluation results be communicated in forms tailored to the specific information needs of different stakeholders? Can the results be disseminated through mass-media outlets? Is this desirable?

If you are evaluating an intervention, do you plan to summarise all your results into a final statement about whether the intervention is good or bad? If so, how will you weigh the different criteria to reflect which criteria are more or less important? Is it possible or desirable to construct a different value summary for each stakeholder group?

of learning outcome is measured. Impact information looks beyond the immediate results to identify long-term effects.

The method of obtaining information will depend on the nature of the information required. A range of methods, from psychometric measurement at one end to interpretive styles at the other, has been developed. Quantitative methods include experiments, surveys, interrupted time-series designs, the Delphi technique and cost analysis. Qualitative methods include case studies, action research and naturalistic and ethnographic approaches. Cronbach[5] advises evaluators to be eclectic in their choice of methods, avoiding slavish adherence to any particular method. Rossi and Freeman[6] advocate the 'good enough' rule for choosing evaluation designs: 'The evaluator should choose the best possible design, taking into account practicality and feasibility...the resources available and the expertise of the evaluator'.

A plethora of evaluation models have been developed that can assist the evaluator in choosing the optimum method for a particular evaluation. These range from comprehensive prescriptions to checklists of suggestions. Each approach comes with its built-in assumptions about evaluation and each emphasises different aspects of evaluation depending on the priorities and preferences of its authors. A few come with careful step-by-step instructions that practitioners can follow, and most are context specific.[7]

Interpreting the findings

Having collected the relevant data, the next stage in evaluation involves its interpretation. Coles and Grant[8] view this process as involving two separate though closely related activities—analysis and explanation.

Methods of analysis are dictated by the form of data collection used. In analysing the findings, it is important to establish the reliability and validity of the data, concepts that have different meanings to quantitative and qualitative practitioners. When both qualitative and quantitative methods are used in the same study, results can be generated that have different implications for the overall conclusion, leading to tension. This may only be resolved after many iterations.[9]

Having analysed the data, the evaluator needs to account for the findings. He or she often needs to interpret the findings, taking into account the theoretical and empirical findings of relevant disciplines, such as psychology, sociology, philosophy, statistics, politics and economics. Because few individuals have expert knowledge of all the fields required, specialist help may be required at this point, which may have further resource implications.

Meta-evaluation

Awareness of the political and social contexts in which evaluation takes place and the limitations of individual methodologies have led to the evolution of meta-evaluation, i.e., evaluation of evaluations. Meta-evaluation aims to improve the quality of evaluations,[10] and may be formative or summative. Formative meta-evaluation aims to improve the evaluation before it is too late. Examples of such methods include: review of research plans by experts and stakeholders, monitoring of the evaluation process by external bodies and independent simultaneous evaluations of the same programme. Summative meta-evaluation can add credibility to final results. Methods include: secondary analyses of collected data, expert review of the findings to determine the validity of the evaluator's interpretations and statements in the final report from personnel involved in the programme.

Dissemination of the findings

Reporting will be in some verbal form, written or spoken, and may be for internal or external consumption. It is important for the evaluator to recognise for which stakeholder group(s) the particular report is being prepared. Evaluators are required to present results in an acceptable and comprehensible way. It is their responsibility to persuade the target audience of the validity and reliability of their results.

A further problem concerns the ethics of reporting. Disseminating information more widely may require censorship; for example, information about a particular teacher would not usually be shared with anyone outside a select audience. The evaluator also has to be aware that the potential ramifications of a report may go wider than anticipated, for instance, into the mass media, which may not be desired.

Influencing decision-making

Coles and Grant[11] suggest the following ways in which evaluators can effect the educational decision-making process:
- involving the people concerned with the educational event at all stages of the evaluation
- helping those who are likely to be associated with the change event to see more clearly for themselves the issues and problems together with putative solutions

- helping people understand how data was interpreted
- establishing appropriate communication channels linking the various groups of people involved
- appointing a coordinator for development, a so-called change agent
- reinforcing natural change; enable use of evaluation to seek out innovations, strengthen them and publicise them further
- promoting further evaluation where innovations have been implemented.

WHAT ARE THE OBVIOUS COSTS OF EVALUATION?

The most obvious cost is the evaluator's time. When evaluators are internal, they will need to be freed from their normal activities to undertake the evaluation. If external, the evaluator's fees will have to be met from the programme budget. They may also require the assistance of various in-house experts whose time would also have to be freed up, or if not available, purchased externally. Other contracted services such as accounting or legal services may also be required. Subcontracts need to be priced as part of budgetary planning. If supplied internally, institutions often include these costs in their overhead rates. The evaluator will require administrative and secretarial support throughout, which if not available internally will have to be purchased.

Depending on the methodologies selected, costs may be incurred for purchasing preexisting evaluation models, questionnaires, attitude or rating scales or other library materials. If preexisting instruments are to be purchased or books or materials ordered, consultation with a librarian or the publisher or author can help in estimating costs.

Specialist equipment such as computer hardware or software may be required as may videotaping or audio equipment. Although many organisations can provide access to computers for data storage and analysis, personal computers or laptops may have to be purchased. Specialist software may also be required for statistical- or qualitative-data analysis. Transcribing of recordings is costly in terms of time (if performed internally) or money (if purchased externally).

Printing and photocopying costs may include preparation of data-collection instruments, reports and other documents. Secretarial staff can be helpful in estimating costs. Discussions with other evaluators who have managed similar projects can also be helpful. Costs of printing and duplicating final reports, binding or any special graphics can be checked with bookbinding and graphic-art companies.

WHAT ARE THE HIDDEN COSTS?

Host organisations (e.g., universities) will have overhead costs, such as facilities and utilities. Most will have fixed percentages of a total budget or of salary costs that they charge as an operating overhead. If applying for external funding, this overhead charge will have to be built into the funding request. However, it is important not to include costs already included in the institution's overhead when costing an evaluation.

Communication costs, including postage and telephone calls, will have to be budgeted for. The cost of surveys can be estimated from the sample size. Fixed costs (e.g., monthly telephone bills or broadband subscriptions) can be budgeted for by multiplying the costs per month by the proposed timescale. Variable costs, such as long-distance phone calls for particular communications, may be estimated based on the context of the evaluation.

Routine materials such as paper and pens may be required if not supplied by the commissioning institution. Routine office estimates should be obtained and costs estimated for the duration of the project.

Travel costs may also have to be met. These will be dependent on the amount of fieldwork and the degree of face-to-face contacts required for designing and conducting the evaluation. These can include mileage for meetings, training, observations, data collection and other activities. Long-distance travel may be required if inspecting similar programmes or disseminating results, and may include airfares, meals and accommodations.

WHAT IS COST-EFFECTIVE EVALUATION?

Often, those responsible for the implementation of an educational programme view resources committed to evaluation as resources lost. Evaluation should be efficient and produce information of sufficient value to justify the resources spent on it. It can be justified only to the extent that it saves resources and/or adds to the quality of the programme. Hodgkinson, Hurst and Levine[12] first introduced the term 'cost-free evaluation' to argue that evaluation can be a means for identifying cost-saving and/or increasing the effectiveness of a programme. Evaluation can help improve productivity and the quality of the programme, either through formative recommendations for improvement that result in a better product and/or lower costs or summative recommendations that result in maintaining or expanding successful, cost-effective educational activities or stopping unsuccessful, costly ones.[13]

To establish cost effectiveness may require analysis of costs and benefits. Undertaking such analysis for educational programmes is often a complex undertaking. A number of approaches exist.[14]

Cost-benefit analysis is only cost-effective when making summative decisions about educational programmes with different outcomes, e.g., in deciding whether to introduce a problem-based learning (PBL) curriculum in a school with an existing traditional curriculum. Each alternative is examined to see whether benefits exceed costs and the ratios of the alternatives are compared. The alternative with the highest benefit-to-cost ratio is selected. This is a value-laden activity, which can result in conflict between the values of the evaluator, the institution and the wider society. It can be difficult to convert costs to monetary terms and even more difficult to convert benefits. Educational benefits are often translated into projected gains in students' knowledge, skills or attitudes. It is important to review the literature to identify commonly accepted benefits and how they are converted into monetary terms. However, it is difficult to translate less obvious benefits, such as students' personal development facilitated by the education process, into monetary terms. It must be remembered that the numbers produced are fallible, and evaluators must produce alternative benefit-to-cost ratios, which take into account different assumptions about costs and benefits.

Cost-effectiveness analysis involves comparing the costs of programmes designed to achieve the same or similar outcomes, e.g., comparing a lecture-based medical ethics course with one using small-group teaching. It also produces results in a ratio. The ratio is expressed as a unit of desired outcome. Unlike cost-benefit analysis, the benefits are not expressed in monetary terms. As many programmes have multiple outcomes, several ratios may be derived, which show the cost of each programme per outcome achieved allowing comparison, e.g., ratios of benefit to cost of improvement in students' ethical sensitivity or improvement in students' knowledge of ethical theory.

Cost-utility analysis involves analysing alternatives by comparing their costs and estimated utility. Estimated utility is a subjective estimate of the probability of a unit-gain, e.g., improvement in exam score. The subjectivity of the method affects its reliability and validity. Its main use is prior to programme implementation. An example of its use would again be prior to the proposed implementation of a PBL curriculum where time and data are limited.

Cost-feasibility analysis is used to determine whether the costs of an alternative, such as a PBL curriculum, prohibit its consideration. The evaluator compares the cost of each alternative and compares it with the available budget. Cost-feasibility studies should be conducted before too much has been invested in programme development.

HOW COULD WE MAKE EVALUATION MORE COST-EFFECTIVE?

With most medical schools facing financial restrictions evaluation is often low down the list of priorities for expenditure. Evaluators can restrict costs by enlisting the services of teachers and other medical staff, administrators, secretarial staff and undergraduate or postgraduate students seeking research experience to assist in the collection and analysis of data. Involving these groups not only helps reduce costs, but also generates interest in the evaluation among stakeholders. However, they may require training and there is a risk of bias if their preexisting perceptions cause them to alter or distort data to fit these perceptions. The evaluator must provide supervision and monitoring throughout, which may make it less economical than it first appears. Local specialists may be used for data collection to reduce travel costs where data needs to be collected at more than one site.

Support materials such as routine questionnaires, records, course documents or previous evaluations may be available. Computer or other information services may also be accessed at little cost. If expensive equipment is required, it may be cheaper to rent than buy. Existing evaluation models may be considered although they are often limited by their context dependency. Evaluation costs may be reduced by 'piggybacking' on other studies where appropriate. Inexpensive data collection methods may be substituted for situations where precision is less important.

Time is an important resource. The evaluator must keep the evaluation on course producing good quality data and analysis while keeping within the proposed time frame. This involves effective planning. Nontechnical, routine tasks may be delegated to less-expensive staff. Knowing when to be ready with results is part of good planning. Limited time can reduce the evaluation's effectiveness as much as a limited budget. If time is an issue, the scope of the evaluation may have to be reduced with parts of the evaluation deferred to a later date.

Services (e.g., long-distance calls or faxes) may be accessed during times when rates are cheaper. In disseminating results using the commissioning institutions, media services can prove cheaper than hiring commercial organisations.

WHAT IS THE COST OF NOT EVALUATING PROPERLY?

With undergraduate medical education alone costing in the region of £1 billion per year in the United Kingdom,[15] it is essential to establish its cost effectiveness. Without proper evaluation the cost effectiveness of medical education would be difficult to determine. It must be recognised, however, that there are a number of situations where evaluation may prove to be of questionable value or even harmful:

- where the evaluation would produce trivial data
- where the results would not be used
- where useful, valid information cannot be produced
- where evaluation is premature for the stage of the programme
- where the propriety of the evaluation is questionable (e.g. where participants could be threatened or harmed).

In these circumstances, the evaluator must persuade the commissioning body why the evaluation should not be attempted. However, such circumstances are uncommon.

The cost of not properly evaluating an educational programme should not be considered in purely financial terms but also from other important perspectives.

- Pragmatic: loss of opportunity to detect poor programmes that not only waste resources, but adversely affect the quality of life of students or produce students whose potential is not reached.
- Ethical: loss of opportunity to detect and challenge unethical practice.

- Social and business: loss of opportunity to discern effective from noneffective programmes.
- Intellectual: loss of opportunity for stakeholder reflection.
- Personal: loss of opportunity to enhance stakeholders' self-esteem.

The question for medical educators considering whether to evaluate is not whether they can afford the cost of evaluation, but can they afford not to?

REFERENCES

1. Popham WJ. *Educational Evaluation.* 2nd ed. Englewood Cliffs, NJ: Prentice Hall; 1988.
2. Cronbach LJ. *Designing Evaluations of Educational and Social Programs.* San Francisco, CA: Jossey-Bass; 1982.
3. Muraskin L. *Understanding Evaluation: the way to better prevention programs.* Rockville, MD: Westat Inc.; 1997.
4. Coles CR, Grant JG. Curriculum evaluation in medical and health-care education. ASME Medical Education Research Booklet 1. *Med Educ.* 1985; **19**: 405.
5. Cronbach LJ. In praise of uncertainty. In: Rossi PH, editor. *Standards for Evaluation Practice.* San Francisco, CA: Jossey-Bass; 1982b. pp. 49–58.
6. Rossi PH, Freeman HE. *Evaluation: a systematic approach.* 3rd ed. Beverly Hills, CA: Sage; 1985.
7. Worthen BL, Sanders JR, Fitzpatrick JL. *Program Evaluation: alternative approaches and practical guidelines.* 2nd ed. New York, NY: Longman; 1997.
8. Coles, Grant, op. cit.
9. Hennigan KM, Flay BR, Cook TD. "Give me the facts!": the use of social science evidence in formulating national policy. In: Kidd RF, Saks MJ, editors. *Advances in Applied Social Psychology.* vol. 1. Hillsdale, NJ: Erlbaum; 1980. pp. 113–48.
10. Worthen, Sanders, Fitzpatrick, op. cit.
11. Coles, Grant, op. cit.
12. Hodgkinson H, Hurst J, Levine H. *Improving and Assessing Performance: evaluation in higher education.* Berkeley, CA: University of California Center for Research and Development in Higher Education; 1975.
13. Worthen, Sanders, Fitzpatrick, op. cit.
14. Ibid.
15. Higher Education Funding Council for England. 2009. Available at: www.hefce.ac.uk/aboutUs/health/funding.htm

CHAPTER 13

Quality assurance systems for medical education

Rodney Gale and Janet Grant

Quality means doing it right when no one is looking.

—Henry Ford

INTRODUCTION

The quality movement owes its origins to the work of Deming[1] who in the late 1940s was concerned with controlling the quality of manufactured goods by statistical sampling at all stages of the production process. His ideas were not widely adopted in the United States but found a home in the booming, postwar manufacturing industries of Japan. Here, the ideas of quality management and quality circles grew and found wide application. A quality circle is a group of workers whose actions interdepend in the production process and who are given time and encouragement to find better ways to produce the desired goods. The ideas came back to the West in the guise of 'continuous quality improvement'. This meant that organisations should constantly be challenging and refining their own best methods of doing things in order to stay one step ahead of the competition.[2] This concept is still alive in the form of organisations seeking to develop quality cultures wherein all employees are striving to improve the quality of the products.[3]

The ideas that were developed in manufacturing soon spread to the service sector where it was helpful to think in production terms about the mechanisms that were underlying the delivery of a service. The classical managerial problem with all services is that the recipient or consumer of the service is an integral part of the delivery of that service; there is no service without customers.[4] Their perception of the service delivered is an important measure of the quality of the service. Thinking has tended to concentrate on those parts of the service delivery that can be objectified as production. For example, there are many actions and processes behind the scenes that enable us to purchase an airline ticket and enjoy a flight. The maintenance of the aircraft, the handling of baggage and the preparation of in-flight catering are just some examples.

Education can be seen as a service industry or to embody many of the attributes of a service industry. As such, it can benefit from the application of quality management techniques. In education, we need to consider quality in both the production side—the creation of the next generation of appropriate medical graduates—and the perceptual side—the maintenance of the values and principles of the medical school or postgraduate organisation. In that Deming was looking for checks and measurements to avoid producing substandard products, the current mode of ensuring that the product of the education process is fit for purpose is substantially equivalent. Whereas manufacture has a product specification detailing the size, weight, dimensions and surface quality of the product, so medical education has a sampling process to assess the quality of educational delivery. Medical education often specifies outcomes and adopts local, national and international standards that determine what a medical graduate should be able to do and how he or she should relate to the professional challenges of medicine.[5]

THE MEANING OF QUALITY

Quality is a word that conveys a range of meanings in its literary use and some of this complexity has strayed into the domain of quality management. We sometimes use quality to denote the very pinnacle of luxury and excess. This could be epitomised among motor vehicles, for instance, by the Rolls-Royce. We also use the term 'quality' to mean that something is very good value for money or is simply very good. The same word is also used to describe the state of reaching a required standard, whether as a manufactured item or a delivered service. A quality product is one that meets its specification. The last element of confusion arises from the nuance of meaning of quality that the product or service is entirely fit for its purpose. This multiplicity of meaning carries over into the terminology and processes that apply in the field of quality management.

Quality control is the term used to ensure that the process, whether manufacture or service delivery, is being faithfully implemented.[6] In manufacture, this would mean the testing of batches and samples throughout the production process, even checking the raw materials to ensure they had the right properties. In medical education, the term could be applied to the process of ensuring that all elements of the curriculum were actually delivered as planned, that the teaching sessions and teaching materials were up to the specified levels and that appropriately qualified students were admitted to the course. The application of quality control involves the identification of key indicators or key metrics that would signal a significant deviation from a planned trajectory. In other words, a curriculum management group would ask themselves how they would know that the process is running smoothly and what signs would tell them that something was going wrong.

Controls assurance[7] is the process whereby the responsible officers of an organisation assure themselves that the quality control variables that will be monitored are, first, in place and activated and, second, provide an adequate set of measures to identify problems. This process is sometimes described as risk-based regulation, since its major concern is with identifying and mitigating risks to the organisation and its operations. Controls assurance developed from the establishment of corporate governance, which was a response to problems within the Board of Guinness, a stock market listed company where the actions of some Board members were not spotted or corrected by the Board as a whole. Earlier versions of corporate governance were a response to the Wall Street crash, whereas most recent interest has centred on the collapse of Enron, a US energy company that was improperly valuing its new supply contracts.

Quality assurance is the process of ensuring that the product or service is fit for its purpose and not just made to the specification.[8] It embodies quality control and continuous process improvement. This means that constant adjustments to the process are made to keep the product relevant to its market. Cars continually evolve and incorporate new features for safety, comfort and entertainment. Modern cars, although essentially motorised boxes on wheels, have come a long way from when the doors needed to be held shut at speeds of over 80 km/hr. The effective medical curriculum continually evolves with subtle changes of emphasis within courses, with the addition of new research results, with the inclusion of new modules and new teaching methods and with responses to changes in national and international standards.

Quality circles are groups of workers, intimately involved in a process, who are given time to meet and discuss how best to improve the process they are engaged in.[9] Quality circles have the authority and resources to make changes. The nearest equivalent, in medical education terms, is the curriculum management group. This body is usually charged with ensuring the smooth running of the curriculum. It seems to fall short of the ideals of quality circles in that there is seldom enough time, power or resources to make the impact necessary.

Quality management is both a description of the quality processes built into the management of a factory, airline, medical school or other organisation, and it is a badge of recognition that the organisation uses the tools of quality to enhance the experience of staff and customers.

Quality culture[10] is very similar to quality management but carries the implication that all parts of the organisation are striving to improve the quality of the service, at all times, often without the explicit actions aimed at quality assurance.

QUALITY IN POSTGRADUATE MEDICAL EDUCATION

Although there is a reasonable case to be made for educational organisations to invest in quality assurance for all their processes, measures of quality have tended to become externalised and now reside mostly in compliance with external standards rather than being driven by internal strategies. Much quality control is aimed at gathering data to support the next inspection visit or to remain compliant with the latest regulatory framework. Quality assurance also seems, all too often, directed at constantly changing the offering to meet modern external standards.

In UK postgraduate education, the body with authority (until April 2010) over the curriculum and the training system was the Postgraduate Medical Education and Training Board (PMETB). It is this body which has approved the content of the specialist training, specified by the royal colleges in their curricula and then provided by National Health Service (NHS) trusts (in primary or secondary care). The process is overseen and managed by the postgraduate deaneries. PMETB devised and implemented a quality assurance framework (QAF)[11] The four aspects of the objectives indicate that its stated intention is to be both a quality control and a quality assurance system. The objectives are as follows:[12]

1 provide public and professional reassurance about the standards and quality of postgraduate medical education in the United Kingdom, through a robust, rigorous set of processes
2 reflect fully the principles of better regulation, demonstrate value for money and be fit for purpose
3 enable improvement and enhancement of the quality of postgraduate medical education
4 ensure specialty focus is maintained at the local and national level by working with the Academy of Medical Royal Colleges, colleges or faculties and postgraduate deaneries.

Behind these objectives is a QAF with five interrelated elements. Behind each element is a further level of detail. For example, one element is standards. This comprises PMETB's 19 standards for curricula and assessment systems, each of which has a large number of detailed components. Very quickly, one arrives at a considerable level of detail. With such detail comes the intrinsic danger that inventiveness, individuality and creativity are hampered. In contrast, the standards set out by the World Federation for Medical Education (WFME)[13] are far less detailed and are specifically designed for local versioning. This approach ensures consistent standards with an incentive to invent, interpret and adapt.

The QAF also has one element relating to a shared evidence base. A positive aspect of this is that data requirements are clearly specified and everyone understands the material they must collect, as a minimum data set. When we drill down to the detail, there are 10 data domains, covering such items as patient safety, diversity, delivery of curriculum and assessment. Each domain yields data items, and there are 40 such data items in all that require routine data gathering. The shared evidence element is also home to the national trainee survey, a massive annual undertaking to record anonymous views about the trainees' perceptions of their training experience.

There are some very positive aspects to such detailed coverage in that it ensures no important elements are missed. On the other hand, the level of detail tends to lend a prescriptive nature that may serve to foster actions that 'fill in the boxes' rather than encourage diversity and creativity in response to the constant challenges of development. In this respect, one could argue that the QAF is weighted towards the quality control aspects, albeit providing a very precise 'manual' to help the user deliver a precise product. The loss of emphasis on aspects of quality assurance and quality improvement may fail to encourage the users to invest in new ways of working and new ways of teaching. Innovation and development tend not to be fostered in such an approach.

QUALITY ASSURANCE IN UNDERGRADUATE MEDICAL EDUCATION

The UK General Medical Council[14] (GMC) sets and monitors standards of undergraduate and preregistration medical education. To ensure that UK medical schools maintain these standards, the GMC provides a quality assurance programme incorporating regular monitoring and visits to schools and their partner institutions.

This programme is known as Quality Assurance of Basic Medical Education (QABME).

It describes itself as a quality assurance programme whose aims are to make sure medical schools meet the outcomes and standards described in *Tomorrow's Doctors*.[15]

This is the publication that describes the knowledge and attributes expected of a modern doctor. The purposes of QABME are described as:

- to identify examples of innovation and good practice
- to identify concerns and help to resolve them
- to identify necessary changes to meet the standards and to set timetables for their implementation
- to promote equality and diversity.

QABME is essentially a self-reporting system backed by an inspection process. Medical schools self-report every year and, as part of the process, are invited to identify problem areas in delivering the desired outcomes and to provide the means to overcome these problems with new controls. In this respect, the QABME process is looking like controls assurance with the GMC acting in the role of the Board and inviting its various departments, in the form of medical schools, to assure it that there will be no surprises.

The refreshing aspect of the QABME system is that it specifically invites innovation and invites medical schools to report on such. It is also far less detailed than the PMETB's QAF system in the way in which the required standards are described. It seems to offer medical schools the encouragement to undertake self-review and to report on the issues that are important to their organisation. The self-review process is a mechanism for initiating change and improvement to the curriculum.

Although self-reporting may have an element of subjectivity, this is countered by the inspection process in the QABME approach, whereby external assessors judge the validity of self-reported findings. Indeed, the major topics for inspection are themselves determined on the basis of issues raised in all the self-reports.

Other medical jurisdictions regulate the production of doctors in slightly different ways, and there are different types of standards in use around the world. Some regulate on outcomes, some on principles, some on objectives and others on risk. This does make for a difficult task in trying to produce a simple cost-benefit approach to the quality assurance process. WFME is a voluntary body that produces international standards, which are widely applied in practice and might eventually become the international benchmark—that would simplify all forms of comparison.

COST-BENEFIT CONSIDERATIONS

It is given that most medical schools would wish to avoid 'failing' a regulatory inspection from an appropriate standard-setting or standards management body. It is difficult to be prescriptive about the nature of failure that is possible, whether a simple yes/no system or one with a wider scale of categories. It is also difficult to assert one model of corrective action that may be prescribed in a given time frame. Finally, it is not possible to compare many systems of specification and quality assurance that are in existence. These conditions make it impossible to produce a single, unified model for cost-benefit analysis of investment in a quality assurance system. For this reason, the following analysis may require considerable adaptation and calibration to make it applicable to differing regulatory regimes and differing organisational circumstances.

The central question remains the same in all aspects of cost-benefit analysis, namely, how much investment is justified to deliver an appropriate proportion of the benefits that will accrue. In this context, we need to consider the full benefits as a starting point.

A well-functioning quality assurance system will embody quality control, the process that ensures that the outcome or product is as it should be by internal and external standards. It will also embrace the thinking on quality improvement that will ensure that the nature of the product specification shifts appropriately for the needs of the trainees, the regulators and the delivery of a healthcare service. What society needs of its healthcare system is constantly evolving and the 'specification' of the trained doctor has to evolve in harmony. The opposite manifests as an inadequate or nonfunctioning quality assurance system and leaves the organisation at risk of failing an inspection. Such a failure may lead to a loss of reputation and influence among peers and potential participants.

The quality control function must sample the teaching and learning activity. This can be by direct observation, by student feedback, by surveys, questionnaires, interviews or any other suitable method. In a complex organisation, the first quality control action is to ensure that the planned activities actually took place, and the students actually participated. The quality control approach covers all aspects of the journey, including selection, mentoring, tutoring, teaching, learning, participation, assessment and examination. Inappropriate systems or actions, at any stage, can lead to the production of a substandard product. Equally, the facilities and services must work in harmony with the overall design specification.

In a typical medical school, it is easy to envisage at least a full-year equivalent volume of work for the quality control function. There will also be the need for support activity to store, process and present the data routinely collected. The quality control function needs immediate data so that corrective action can be taken, where necessary. For illustrative purposes, we can assume that a further half-year full-time equivalent input will be required. These are constant and invariant costs.

The quality assurance role is best discharged through more thoughtful self-reviews. These are a little like inspection visits from regulators but are undertaken by organisations themselves. They go beyond checking that the training processes are working and seek to ensure that the 'product' is appropriate. Self-review can include everything from an individual module to a departmental input to the whole syllabus and the curriculum itself. Anything can be reviewed—from the content, to the teaching and learning methods, to the mode of delivery, the facilities and the support functions. The process involves a critical look at the current activities and an appraisal of alternative ideas emerging from within the organisation, from local competitors and from national and international sources. Health needs vary around the world, and the nature of health workers varies with them. Again, we cannot prescribe the contents of self-review. The process should be more than ensuring compliance with external standards and should embody innovation and exploration of novel approaches.

A small team can provide the quality control input, with contributory help from a larger number of other faculty members. The quality assurance part has to involve a larger steering group to ensure that all major stakeholders have adequate representation and have some degree of ownership of any changes that may arise from the review. It is important to recognise that there will be considerable data retrieval and analysis required to underpin proposed changes. Specific work groups will need to be assigned specific tasks within the review process.

For illustration, we could assume a steering group of 10 people, each putting in the equivalent of 2 weeks full-time work and 30 people in work groups putting in similar effort. This amounts to 80 weeks or 1.5 years, in round terms. We can also assume that this effort occurs equally every year, although it will probably vary considerably in practice. The overall quality assurance system thus costs considerable amount of faculty effort each year.

Having established some sort of cost structure, we need to review the benefits. These depend somewhat on the strategic intentions of the organisation. One wishing to be a leading light and attract the brightest trainees would reap benefits by continuing to attract and retain the brightest, who would perform well in examinations or assessments, increase the organisation's reputation further and contribute to a positive spiral. Any setback would have a large impact on the life of the organisation. The brightest students may go elsewhere, the leading faculty may do likewise and there may be remedial effort required to try to rectify the problems.

An organisation aiming to serve its local community may still feel the effects of failing to undertake sufficient quality assurance activity. Perhaps the output quality may fall so that the trainees or students do not get the jobs they desire and future generations look elsewhere for training. Perhaps the quality of trainees falls so that they represent a possible danger to the health of the local population. Perhaps the content of the course can get out of synchrony with the health needs of the region and the organisation could lose political support or economic support.

These effects are very difficult to quantify but could be profound. Even at a less severe level of impact, they could cause the organisation to have to exert additional effort to put matters right. The effort has to come from somewhere, so either their costs will rise or they will have to divert resources from some other activity, such as research.

Detailed methods of calculating the ratio of costs-to-benefits are presented in Chapter 10 on curriculum design and will not be repeated here.

Table 13.1 presents very approximate costs for a quality assurance system and lists some of the benefits, purely as a guide. If followed in practice, a cost or value can be placed on the items in the benefit column.

TABLE 13.1 Costs and benefits of a quality assurance system

Costs of a quality assurance system	Benefits of investment in quality assurance
For quality control 1 year equivalent faculty lead 0.5 year equivalent data gathering	Ensures preparedness for external inspections Generates appetite for review and reform Maintains external reputation
For quality assurance 1.5 year equivalent faculty input Total cost: 3 year equivalent	Safeguards income Avoids costly remedial activity

CONCLUSIONS

All organisations providing medical education, whether undergraduate or postgraduate, can benefit from investing in a quality assurance process. It is essential to have quality control to ensure that the educational machine is running well, but it is also important to have the quality assurance process that ensures that the product is fit for purpose, evolving and not just well-produced.

REFERENCES

1. Deming WE. *Elementary Principles of the Statistical Control of Quality*. Tokyo: Nippon Kagaku Gijutsu Renmei; 1950, 1952; in English; Deeming WE. *Out of the Crisis*. MIT Press; 1986.
2. Draugalis JR, Slack MK. A continuous quality improvement model for developing innovative instructional strategies. *Am J Pharm Educ.* 1999; **63**: 354–8; Shortell SM, O'Brien JL, Carman JM, *et al.* Assessing the impact of continuous quality improvement/total quality management: concept versus implementation. *Health Serv Res.* 1995; **30**(2): 377–401; Kalzuny AD, McLaughlin CP, Kibbe DC. Continuous quality improvement in the clinical setting; enhancing adoption. *Qual Manag Health Care.* 1992; **1**(1): 37–44.
3. Ehlers UD. Understanding quality culture. *Qual Assur Educ.* 2009; **17**(4): 343–63.
4. Lovelock C, Wright L. *Principles of Service Marketing and Management*. NJ: Prentice-Hall; 1998.
5. *Tomorrow's Doctors*. London: GMC Publications; 2009. Available at: www.gmc-uk.org/education/undergraduate/tomorrows_doctors_2009_foreword.asp (accessed 21 June 2010).
6. Wikipedia offers a reasonable definition. www.en.wikipedia.org/wiki/Quality_assurance (accessed 21 June 2010).
7. HSC 2001/005 Governance in the new NHS: controls assurance statements 2000/2001 and establishment of controls assurance unit. London, UK: Department of Health; 2001.
8. Wikipedia, op. cit.
9. See *Kaizen and Total Quality Management (TQM)*, for example, at www.1000ventures.com/business_guide/mgmt_kaizen_tqc_main.html (accessed 21 June 2010).
10. Ehlers, op. cit.
11. See the PMETB website. Available at: www.pmetb.org.uk (accessed 21 June 2010).
12. Ibid.
13. See the World Federation for Medical Education website. Available at: www3.sund.ku.dk/ (accessed 21 June 2010).
14. See the General Medical Council website. Available at: www.gmc-uk.org/education/undergraduate/qabme_programme.asp (accessed 21 June 2010).
15. *Tomorrow's Doctors*, op. cit.

CHAPTER 14

Research into cost effectiveness in medical education

Melanie Calvert

Money won't buy happiness, but it will pay the salaries of a large research staff to study the problem.

—Bill Vaughan

INTRODUCTION

In this chapter, we consider how the medical education community should prioritise research into cost effectiveness in medical education, which costs and outcomes may be considered in cost-effectiveness analyses, research methods for assessing cost effectiveness and how this can be achieved in practice.

WHAT RESEARCH IS NEEDED?

We need to ensure that medical education at both undergraduate and postgraduate level is evidence based and effective. In a constrained environment, we also need to ensure that any new developments are cost-effective, in the long term, providing the greatest benefit in health per unit cost of training.[1,2]

There has been an increase over the past four decades in the number of publications assessing medical education interventions; however, 'considerable opportunities for improvement remain' within the medical education research arena, and estimates of associated costs are vanishingly rare.[3]

Given the scarcity of robust evidence of cost-effective medical education, there is a wide scope for activity.[4] Because education research also incurs a cost, researchers would be wise to target areas where students, and ideally patients, may gain the greatest benefits or, alternatively, those which incur the greatest costs. Some education approaches may have a large impact on budget compared with traditional methods and, therefore, need to demonstrate improved outcomes for students to warrant widespread introduction. Some education initiatives (e.g., using portfolios as a competency assessment) are extremely costly in terms of tutor and student time.[5] Alternative methods for attainment of the same outcomes may be considered on efficiency grounds.

Much of the research in medical education has been focused on undergraduates, but it is clear that practical training and competency assessment in the workplace also need to be effective.[6,7] Despite substantial funding for continuing professional development (CPD), there has been limited evaluation of the cost effectiveness of CPD programmes.[8,9]

ASSESSING COST EFFECTIVENESS

To assess cost effectiveness, we need to compare education outcomes with costs. However, which costs and outcomes are appropriate and measurable?

What costs?

'The cost of implementing a new teaching approach will vary based on perspective'.[10] Ideally, we would like to know the costs and benefits to society. However, the reality is that assessing costs to society is complex. For example, 'from a societal view, we may argue that graduate entry courses are cost-inefficient, given the additional resources and training involved. However, the tantalising question remains: what are the benefits to society of this additional education of graduates who are older and often more mature than their younger counterparts?'[11,12]

A more accessible approach is to capture the costs accrued from the perspective of the medical school or college, which will include: curriculum development, preparation, delivery and assessment costs, and may reflect educator costs and physical inputs such as the learning environment and materials.[13] This is analogous to the approach used by organisations such as the National Institute for Health and Clinical Excellence (NICE) that appraise new interventions on the basis of their costs to the healthcare system (National Health Service and social services).[14] This is simpler than trying to include all costs incurred by the individual and society (such as travel, additional care or time off-work).

Costs may be viewed in monetary terms or in terms of student or educator time. Using either approach, we need to consider the opportunity cost, i.e., the costs of an action in terms of the alternatives forgone as a consequence.[15] We need to maximise limited time and resources to maximise care and beneficial outcomes for patients.

Measuring effectiveness: choice of an appropriate outcome measure

One immediate challenge that faces us is the choice of an appropriate outcome measure. The ultimate aim of medical education should be to improve the health or well-being of patients.[16] Measuring student views, perceptions or attitudes may be relatively straightforward, but, as yet, there is little evidence that a positive effect on student views will lead to improved delivery of care or patient health. Wherever possible, we should strive to select outcomes that are likely to reflect subsequent practice. It may be tempting to have a host of primary outcomes, but this should be avoided. Including several outcome measures raises 'the problem that the likelihood of finding a statistically significant result by chance alone increases with the number of tests undertaken'.[17] The primary outcome for a study ideally should be reliable and valid, and also sensitive to change, but further work is needed to develop robust outcomes for pedagogic research.

MEASURING COST EFFECTIVENESS

In general, new approaches may be more costly (or of equal cost), but we may hope for improved outcomes. In such cases, we are interested in the incremental cost-effectiveness ratio, i.e., the additional cost of one unit of outcome gained because of a new educational method, when compared with the alternative. The incremental cost-effectiveness ratio can be viewed on a cost-effectiveness plane (*see* Figure 14.1). The incremental costs are positive above the horizontal axis and negative below the

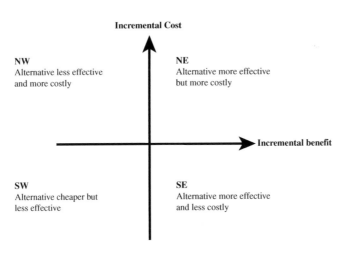

NE = northeast quadrant; NW = northwest quadrant;
SE = southeast quadrant; SW = southwest quadrant.

FIGURE 14.1 Incremental costs and benefits

horizontal axis. The incremental effects of the new education initiative are positive to the right of the vertical axis and negative to the left of the vertical axis.

A new education approach that is cheaper than the traditional approach and leads to improved outcomes (southeast quadrant) is viewed as dominant and cost-effective, whereas if the new approach is more costly and less effective (northwest quadrant), it is cost-inefficient.[18] The southwest and northeast quadrants offer trade-offs between costs and effects that would need to be carefully considered to inform curriculum development. In all cases, it is necessary to consider the level of uncertainty around any estimates to inform decision-making.

WHAT CAN WE LEARN FROM THE HEALTHCARE SETTING?

Just as in healthcare, finite resources and increasing costs lead to inevitable rationing in medical education. We may choose to ration based solely on current opinion and belief or choose a more robust approach.

Educationalists may bemoan the difficulties in evaluating education, but the challenges are not unique to education, and we can learn much from the extensive research and methodological advances in healthcare evaluation. In pharmaceutical trials, common limitations and challenges faced by policy makers include: a focus on intermediate outcomes that do not reflect 'real world' practice, and lack of generalisability due to selective inclusion criteria and short-term duration, making it difficult to assess issues such as long-term effects (such as long-term safety). These challenges can equally be seen as the challenges facing pedagogic research where surrogate outcomes such as measures of student performance in the short term may be the only reasonable proxy available for longer term benefits in the provision of care and health of their patients.

Methods used for health-technology assessment to inform national health policy, such as randomised controlled trials (RCTs), meta-analysis and model-based approaches, may be useful tools in developing evidence-based (cost) effective medical education.[19,20,21]

RANDOMISED CONTROLLED TRIALS

One way that we can assess the incremental cost effectiveness of a new medical initiative compared with the standard approach is through a within-trial cost-effectiveness analysis. RCTs are currently underutilised in medical education to assess effectiveness or cost effectiveness.[22,23] Randomisation protects us from the potential bias and confounding that we may observe in case–control or cohort studies. It ensures that differences in outcome are due to the play of chance or the education strategy. Most medical schools enrol large numbers of students, which could potentially provide robust estimates using such an approach. Costs associated with different pedagogic approaches, which may be money or time, can be quantified during a trial alongside results of assessment to enable within-trial cost-effectiveness analyses.

RCTs in medical education are not without their challenges. We may regard education as a complex intervention, effect sizes may be small, and if a non-inferiority design is to be used, then large sample sizes may be necessary.[24,25] A further challenge with such an approach is ensuring that students are not disadvantaged because of the research. This is of notable importance if the primary outcome is a summative assessment that may significantly impact on success in higher education or future career progression. One way to avoid this problem would be to use formative assessment as the primary outcome and to offer students access to the alternative method of learning following the trial but before summative assessment. Cross-over trial designs may also help to avoid such problems.

LARGE EPIDEMIOLOGICAL STUDIES

An alternative to the RCT is to undertake a large cohort study. For example, it may be tempting to try and assess the costs and outcomes in consecutive years before and after the implementation of a new teaching method. This may be appealing because it overcomes some of the practical problems encountered in a trial such as ensuring students are not disadvantaged through the research. Although such studies may be extremely useful in evaluating the relationship between student characteristics and performance in assessment, they are not best placed to evaluate the impact of an intervention or its cost effectiveness (e.g., alternative methods of teaching) due to the risk of confounding. Several changes may occur in a curricula or assessment from year to year as will student case-mix, thus making any differences in outcome difficult to attribute to a single intervention.

PROGNOSTIC MODELS

There is evidence in the medical literature to suggest that students with certain characteristics outperform their peers (these characteristics may include gender, overseas status, graduate entry versus mainstream students).[26,27] With a wide range of learning styles, backgrounds and experiences, we may expect certain students to benefit more from certain pedagogic approaches. Using prognostic models, we can evaluate in which subgroup of students different approaches are more likely to be cost-effective. Work by Harrell *et al.* and a recent series in the *British Medical Journal* may provide a useful starting point for those interested in such an approach.[28,29,30,31] Results of such models may allow students to receive a more tailored approach to teaching or assessment.

THE FUTURE: META-ANALYSIS AND MODEL-BASED APPROACHES?

Pooling results from several RCTs of equivalent pedagogic approaches using meta-analysis[32,33] provide a greater number of students on which to estimate the effect of a new education approach compared with standard practice—resulting in greater statistical power and precision. This combined estimate of the intervention effect may be used to inform cost-effectiveness analysis. Currently, using meta-analysis to assess medical education is limited, but existing studies demonstrate the potential of such an approach.[34,35,36]

Decision analytic models are also widely used in the evaluation of health technologies. This approach uses mathematical techniques 'to obtain a clearer understanding of the relationships between incremental costs and their consequences'.[37] A variety of techniques may be used, including decision-tree-modelling. Such models allow specification of a range of scenarios of interest[38] and would allow us to combine information such as student demographics with evidence of the effectiveness (from RCTs or meta-analysis) and cost of different modes of education. The results could be used to inform curriculum development or postgraduate training. Such models could be used to assess the incremental cost effectiveness of a new education initiative compared with the standard approach for different subgroups of students, such as European Union or overseas students, or those with previous learning experience such as graduate entry versus mainstream students. Through adjustment of parameter estimates such as student characteristics that are known to be associated with an outcome, a model-based approach could potentially be used to predict effects in medical schools throughout the United Kingdom or even abroad.

PRACTICALITIES OF ASSESSING COST EFFECTIVENESS

Ethical issues

There has been a recent shift in medical education research with increased emphasis on the need for formal ethical review.[39] Institutional review should be undertaken at a minimum to ensure that any potential risks and benefits that students may face have been considered. In medicine, examination failures may have serious implications for future career progression and financial state. Great care must therefore be taken to ensure that students are not disadvantaged by cost-effectiveness research. Some information for medical education research is already routinely collected (such as examination scores); however, the approaches described earlier to assess cost effectiveness may necessitate completion of additional questionnaires or even additional assessments to assess costs and outcomes. Medical schools should have a clear overview of all medical education research activities to ensure that students are not overburdened or disadvantaged.

Multi-disciplinary research team

Research into the cost effectiveness of medical education will necessitate an experienced multidisciplinary team. Ideally, this would comprise not only experienced

educationalists but also a statistician and/or health economist with the necessary trial or epidemiology experience, and perhaps an ethicist and qualitative researcher. These may not need to be solely dedicated to cost-effectiveness research, but such work could complement other research and teaching activities in higher education.

Proof of concept studies may be simpler to undertake at a single university or site. However, for confirmatory studies, a multicentre approach should be considered and adopted where feasible and appropriate. Standardisation across medical schools means that many questions are common across institutions and could be answered to provide results generalisable at a national level.

Funding

Funding may be viewed as a barrier to medical education research activities. Cost-effectiveness research is likely to incur additional costs in terms of data collection and analysis. Universities may choose to use core funds to support such activities; however, trialists, statisticians and epidemiologists with the necessary skills may face conflicts in supporting such 'in-house' research rather than seeking external funding for medical research.[40] Obtaining programme grants from the Higher Education Academy or a series of small-scale grants from other external funders may help to overcome this.

CONCLUSIONS

We should not simply implement new assessment methods, clinical simulations and other recent developments without evidence of impact on student learning and outcomes (ideally patient care). It is unlikely to be practical, or even the best use of resources to undertake a formal cost-effectiveness analysis of each curriculum development, but the fact that so many costly innovations (in terms of time and money) are readily introduced without robust assessment seems naïve. Research-led higher education institutions are uniquely placed to lead developments in this area, but staffs need to be encouraged and gain recognition for such endeavours. The methods described earlier can and should be used where feasible to assess the effectiveness and cost effectiveness of alternative approaches to teaching and assessment. Interpretive investigation should also be undertaken to complement the positivist approaches described earlier. This would allow us to explore and hopefully understand why certain students are more or less likely to benefit from new education initiatives, thus allowing us to support the diverse needs of our students in an effective and efficient way.

ACKNOWLEDGEMENTS

Thanks to Nick Freemantle for his advice on this chapter.

REFERENCES

1. Calvert MJ, Freemantle N. Cost-effective undergraduate medical education? *J R Soc Med.* 2009; **102**(2): 46–8.
2. Palmer S, Byford S, Raftery J. Economics notes: types of economic evaluation. *BMJ.* 1999; **318**(7194): 1349.
3. Baernstein A, Liss HK, Carney PA, *et al.* Trends in study methods used in under-graduate medical education research, 1969–2007. *JAMA.* 2007; **298**(9): 1038–45.
4. Ibid.
5. Buckley S, Coleman J, Davison I, *et al.* The educational effects of portfolios on undergraduate student learning: a best evidence medical education (BEME) system-atic review. BEME Guide No. 11. *Med Teach.* 2009; **31**(4): 282–98.
6. Belfield C, Brown C, Thomas H, *et al. Cost-effective Continuing Professional Development in the NHS – report to the Department of Health.* London: Department of Health; 2001. pp. 1–85.
7. Brown CA, Belfield CR, Field SJ. Cost effectiveness of continuing professional devel-opment in health care: a critical review of the evidence. *BMJ.* 2002; **324**(7338): 652–5.
8. Belfield, *et al., op. cit.*
9. Brown, Belfield, Field, op. cit.
10. Calvert, Freemantle, op. cit.
11. Ibid.
12. Jauhar S. From all walks of life – nontraditional medical students and the future of medicine. *N Engl J Med.* 2008; **359**(3): 224–7.
13. Buckley, *et al., op. cit.*
14. National Institute for Clinical Excellence. Available at: www.nice.org.uk/aboutnice/whatwedo/what_we_do jsp (accessed 2009).
15. Palmer S, Raftery J. Economics notes: opportunity cost. *BMJ.* 1999; **318**(7197): 1551–2.
16. Freeth D, Hammick M, Koppel I, *et al.* Occasional paper no. 2: a critical review of evaluations of interprofessional education. *Higher Educ Acad.* 2002; 1–68. Available at: www.health.ltsn.ac.uk/publications/occasionalpaper/occasionalpaper02.pdf (accessed 24 June 2010).
17. Freemantle N. Interpreting the results of secondary end points and subgroup analy-ses in clinical trials: should we lock the crazy aunt in the attic? *BMJ.* 2001; **322**(7292): 989–91.
18. Fenwick E, Marshall D, Levy A, *et al.* Using and interpreting cost-effectiveness accept-ability curves: an example using data from a trial of management strategies for atrial fibrillation. *BMC Health Serv Res.* 2006; **6**(1): 52.
19. Calvert, Freemantle, op. cit.
20. Hutchinson L. Evaluating and researching the effectiveness of educational interven-tions. *BMJ.* 1999; **318**(7193): 1267–9.
21. Carney PA, Nierenberg DW, Pipas CF, *et al.* Educational epidemiology: applying population-based design and analytic approaches to study medical education. *JAMA.* 2004; **292**(9): 1044–50.
22. Baernstein, *et al., op. cit.*
23. Hutchinson, op. cit.

24. Craig P, Dieppe P, Macintyre S, *et al.* Developing and evaluating complex interventions: the new Medical Research Council guidance. *BMJ.* 2008; **337**: a1655.
25. Norman G. RCT = results confounded and trivial: the perils of grand educational experiments. *Med Educ.* 2003; **37**: 582–4.
26. Hutchinson, op. cit.
27. Calvert M, Ross N, Freemantle N, *et al.* Examination performance of graduate entry medical students compared to mainstream students. *J R Soc Med.* 2009 Oct; **102**(10): 425–30.
28. Hutchinson, op. cit.
29. Harrell FE, Lee KL, Mark DB. Multivariable prognostic models: issues in developing models, evaluating assumptions and adequacy, and measuring and reducing errors. *Stat Med.* 1996; **15**: 361–87.
30. Hutchinson, op. cit.
31. Moons KGM, Royston P, Vergouwe Y, *et al.* Prognosis and prognostic research: what, why, and how? *BMJ.* 2009; **338**: b375.
32. Hutchinson, op. cit.
33. Egger M, Smith GD, Phillips AN. Meta-analysis: principles and procedures. *BMJ.* 1997; **315**(7121): 1533–7.
34. Forsetlund L, Bjørndal A, Rashidian A, *et al.* Continuing education meetings and workshops: effects on professional practice and health care outcomes. *Cochrane Database Syst Rev.* 2009; **15**(2): CD003030.
35. Davis DA, Mazmanian PE, Fordis M, *et al.* Accuracy of physician self-assessment compared with observed measures of competence: a systematic review. *JAMA.* 2006; **296**(9): 1094–102.
36. Best Evidence Medical Education. Available at: www2.warwick.ac.uk/fac/med/beme/ (accessed 24 June 2010).
37. Decision analytic modelling in the economic evaluation of health technologies: a consensus statement. *Pharmacoeconomics.* 2000; **17**(5): 443–4.
38. Philips Z, Bojke L, Sculpher M, *et al.* Good practice guidelines for decision-analytic modelling in health technology assessment: a review and consolidation of quality assessment. *Pharmacoeconomics.* 2006; **24**(4): 355.
39. Cate O. Why the ethics of medical education research differs from that of medical research. *Med Educ.* 2009; **7**: 608–10.
40. Parry J, Mathers J, Thomas H, *et al.* More students, less capacity? An assessment of the competing demands on academic medical staff. *Med Educ.* 2008; **42**(12): 1155–65.

CHAPTER 15

Cost effectiveness in medical education: conclusion and next steps

Kieran Walsh

I hate quotations. Tell me what you know.

—*Ralph Waldo Emerson*

Medical education is an expensive business. It is also an important one and if nothing else the previous chapters show that the issue of cost effectiveness in medical education is complex. There are no immediate and obvious answers nor, in many cases, is there an obvious way to frame problems or an obvious route forward.

In the undergraduate arena, where curricula are large and run over a period of time, one potential cost-effectiveness strategy is to identify components of the curriculum on which to focus. Reducing the duration of courses will certainly save costs—as long as strong checks are in place to ensure that the highest standards of quality are still upheld. Another obvious factor to look at is student attrition. If students withdraw from the course before completing it, then the funding spent on the medical education to that point is likely to be wasted. Self-directed learning is likely to be effective if executed properly and may save costs; similarly, collaboration in the form of interprofessional education or interinstitutional sharing of resources. As Finucane and McCrorie state 'considerations of cost effectiveness do not yet feature highly on the reform agenda in medical education; the inexorable rise of consumerism means that this is soon likely to change. One of the major new challenges for undergraduate medical educators is to reduce costs while producing competent medical graduates'. Standing still is no longer an option.

In the area of postgraduate medical education, cost effectiveness is important but can only be achieved if we know what we are producing and how much it costs to produce it. However, at present, there is a paucity of data on both of these metrics. So, there needs to be research to answer the key questions posed by Thakore, namely 'what is the best curriculum to develop future specialists, how can this curriculum be delivered and assessed and how can we support the deliverers of this process'. Thakore's point about always remembering the patient when considering cost effectiveness in medical education is also well made. All too often in the past, the patient has been a useful if silent prop in our medical education endeavours—we must never cut education costs in ways that may lead to deterioration in patient care.

The concept of cost-effective continuing professional development (CPD) is even more challenging. As Sandars outlines 'measuring the cost effectiveness of CPD will be a major challenge since identifying the true costs of educational interventions and deciding on the appropriate expected benefits that are relevant to all stake-holders is not easy'. There will no doubt be resistance to the very idea that the cost effectiveness of CPD needs to be examined, but if significant amounts of CPD are to continue to be funded by the taxpayer, then the same payer will want to ensure that CPD 'is value for money and that time on CPD activities can produce tangible changes in professional behaviours and ultimately improved clinical care'.

Nestel *et al.* similarly found few studies of the cost effectiveness of interprofessional education (IPE). They claim that 'general statements about cost effectiveness of IPE are meaningless because of the wide variability in costs and outcomes associated with the diverse nature of IPE activities'. However, they do move purposefully from the general to the specific and cite the study by Hansen *et al.* on the cost effectiveness of treating patients undergoing management and rehabilitation for primary hip and knee replacement procedures in an interprofessional training unit or a conventional ward.[1] Clinical outcomes in both units were similar, but the IPE unit seemed to be more cost-effective. Perhaps the way forward will lie in similar small and well-defined studies of this kind.

At face value, many would conclude that online learning must be more cost-effective than traditional face-to-face education. There are no travel or subsistence or accommodation costs—for learner or teacher. Learning can take place in the workplace and at a time and place that suits the learner. However, nowhere is the issue of hidden costs more important than in online learning. People take the software and hardware and even electricity for granted but they all cost money. The learning programmes themselves need to be developed and can be expensive if they are high quality. More cost-effectiveness analyses is needed in the field of online learning—but some good news is that online learning is perhaps more easily tracked than other forms of learning, and as a result, its cost and effectiveness may be easier to measure.

In face-to-face learning, what evidence does exist may be surprising to some. For years, certain educationalists have announced the 'death of the lecture', but this most traditional of educational methods is still defying its critics. However, as Spencer and Pearson say, a 'good lecturer will actively engage learners using a variety of techniques, intuitively model professional attitudes and thinking, and will link theory and practice and bring concepts to life through stories. They will communicate enthusiasm for the subject, provide a scaffold on which learners can construct new knowledge, stimulate further inquiry and may actually be more up-to-date than other sources of information, such as textbooks or even the internet, indeed may provide information not available from other sources'.

And lectures can be cost effective. According to Brown and Belfield, 'based on experimental evidence, there is no mode of education that is more clearly cost-effective than lectures for imparting information'.[2]

Moving from the traditional to the modern, as Ker *et al.* state, 'simulation is a costly, but effective way of ensuring reliable standards of practice are in place across the healthcare sector'. Simulation allows learners to make and learn from mistakes in safe environments without harming patients—a concept that all will sign up to. And yet it does not always have to be expensive. While simulated emergency rooms and even simulated hospitals naturally tend to the more expensive end of the scale, communication skills can be taught in a side room with a learner, an actor/patient and a facilitator. In the past, simulation has been the reserve of selected special-ists like anaesthetists and resuscitation officers, but it is becoming mainstream and being taken up by everyone from GPs to psychiatrists—who will not need expensive kit but rather some time, some space and some good facilitation skills.

The chapter on problem-based learning (PBL) deliberately asks the question: is a cost-effective approach possible? This title recognises the inherent costs of the problem-based approach, but according to Wittert and Nelson, 'the most cost-effective approach to the implementation and maintenance of PBL in any particular medical school will depend on the staffing and organisational structure in place and the balance between research and teaching being undertaken by these staff members'. They state that 'programmes that utilise existing academic staff will find that the costs of establishing and maintaining PBL are less than those programmes that employ casual tutors whose payments will need to be absorbed over and above what is already being paid in salaries to academic staff. So, although much work still needs to be done, there is cause for some cautious optimism.

Cost-effective curriculum design as a concept is not a simple one. As Grant and Gale explain, 'the variety of medical schools and the variety of curriculum models with differing intensities of faculty involvement make exact quantification almost impossible, even for the direct and indirect costs and benefits that are felt at the institutional level'. As they state, 'to use cost-benefit analysis as a precise decision tool would require attention to calculating the costs of inadequacies in curriculum design to the broader society of the medical school and to the healthcare systems themselves'. Clearly, there is some way to go here.

When looking at cost-effective assessment, Schuwirth and van der Vleuten take a simple and yet eloquent approach. In their chapter, they highlight some of the major sources of cost-ineffective practices in assessment, such as the belief in expensive methods, inefficient sampling and unnecessary long observations. At a simple level, if these cost-inefficient practices are eliminated, then it is likely that institutions will spend less on assessment and that the funds that they do spend will be spent more wisely.

Evaluation is another area where efficiencies can be made in processes that will undoubtedly reduce costs. However, evaluation already often comes far down the list of spending priorities, and there is a risk with overemphasis on cost effectiveness that it falls off the end of the list altogether. As Goldie says, we should keep in mind the financial and human costs of not evaluating properly—not least 'the loss of opportunity to detect poor programmes that not only waste resources but adversely affect the quality of life of students or produce students whose potential is not reached'.

Quality assurance, a natural relation of evaluation, does cost in terms of both staff and money but it does result in significant benefits, not least in that it 'ensures preparedness for external inspections, generates appetite for review and reform, maintains external reputation, safeguards income and avoids costly remedial activity'.

Further work is certainly needed before we will know more about cost effectiveness in medical education, and yet perhaps we do not need stand-alone cost-effectiveness studies so much as the integration of cost effectiveness into studies that are happening anyway. So, in future, if a researcher is to look at a new method of medical education, they should at the very least look at the costs of the innovation compared with the costs of more traditional methods.

If and when cost effectiveness in medical education as a concept starts to come of age, then difficult decisions will have to be taken. If a new form of education is shown to be more effective and less expensive, then it will have to be taken up and the old method gradually discontinued. Too often in the past, new educational interventions of proven benefit have been slow to be taken up and traditional less-effective methods have continued—this must not be allowed to happen in this field.

The way forward in cost effectiveness in medical education lies with everyone involved in medical education. Lecturers in medical education or medical educational researchers will have a key role to play—but all tutors and teachers and supervisors should also play a role. It is a challenging field, but if we don't come up with our own solutions, then solutions may be imposed from above and may come from those with the least experience in medical education who are least well placed to make decisions.

It is traditional for the final paragraph of the final chapter to sum up by saying that more research is needed. This may be the case but there is no doubt that we can already hang our hats on some principles and take certain actions. Some such principles are quite basic and do not really need research to prove that they would be effective. They are best demonstrated through simple examples. For instance, a GP in the United Kingdom flying to a southern European city in June to sit though a series of lectures on tropical disease is unlikely to be applying best practice in cost-effective education. This approach is likely to be expensive, and the content and format of the education may not meet his specific learning needs. The same goes for a physician who books into a meeting at the last minute (and thus pays a premium price) as he wants to fulfill his annual learning credits quota. These examples seem so obvious as to be almost crass, and yet poor practice continues to this day. Discussing and working through clinical problems with colleagues during a coffee break at work is likely to be both more effective and economic. Will learning in the workplace, for the workplace and during workplace hours become Yeats' 'best modern way' of the future?

REFERENCES

1. Hansen T, Jacobsen F, Larsen K. An evaluation of a training unit in Denmark. *J Interprof Care.* 2009; **23**: 234–42.
2. Belfield CR, Brown CA. How cost-effective are lectures? A review of the experimental evidence. In: Levin HM, McEwan PJ, editors. *Cost-Effectiveness and Educational Policy. AEFA Handbook.* Larchmont, NJ: Eye on Education; 2002.

Index